# UPHOLSTERING & RECOVERING

*Created and designed by*
*the editorial staff of*
*ORTHO BOOKS*

*Project Director*
Karin Shakery

*Writers*
Janette Hall
Carol Henderson
Karin Shakery

*Illustrator*
Edith Allgood

*Photographer*
Kit Morris

# Ortho Books

*Publisher*
Robert J. Dolezal

*Editorial Director*
Christine Robertson

*Production Director*
Ernie S. Tasaki

*Managing Editors*
Michael D. Smith
Sally W. Smith

*System Manager*
Katherine L. Parker

*National Sales Manager*
Charles H. Aydelotte

*Marketing Specialist*
Dennis M. Castle

*Operations Assistant*
Georgiann Wright

*Distribution Specialist*
Barbara F. Steadham

*Admininstrative Assistant*
Francine Lorentz-Olson

*Senior Technical Analyst*
J. A. Crozier, Jr., PhD.

Address all inquiries to
Ortho Books
Chevron Chemical Company
Consumer Products Division
Box 5047
San Ramon, CA 94583

ISBN 0-89721-087-5
Library of Congress Catalog Card Number 86-72434

**Chevron Chemical Company**
6001 Bollinger Canyon Road, San Ramon, CA 94583

# Special Thanks
Lonnie & David Hinckley
Guy Chaddock & Company
San Francisco, Calif.

Paul Bianculli & Steve Copeland
The Upholstery Connection
San Francisco, Calif.

# Designers & Showrooms
Guy Chaddock & Company
San Francisco, Calif.
Pages 1, 6 (bottom), 9 (center right), 64–65, 79, 85, 91

Dawn McKenna ASID
for Decorators Walk
San Francisco, Calif.
Pages 27, 84, 87, 88

Designers Showroom III
San Francisco, Calif.
Page 6 (top)

Ginny Hopper
Hopper Interiors
San Francisco, Calif.
Pages 64–65, 77, 89, 90

Kroll Furniture
San Francisco, Calif.
Pages 17, 19 (bottom right)

Christie McRae
C. L. McRae
San Francisco, Calif.
Pages 1, 64–65

Pacific Atlas Woodworking Company
San Francisco, Calif.
Page 22

Tony Pisacane (Cabinetry)
San Francisco, Calif.
Page 80

Syrie Moughan for
Randolph & Hein, Inc.
San Francisco, Calif.
Pages 9 (center), 21

Recover Me
San Francisco, Calif.
Pages 74–75, 76, 77

R. Jones Associates for
Shears & Windows
San Francisco, Calif.
Pages 9 (top and bottom), 71

Stockfleth-Disston
San Francisco, Calif.
Page 8

The Upholstery Connection
San Francisco, Calif.
Pages 50–51, 64–65, 78, 83 (top and bottom), 93

*Front cover.* A beautifully smooth, scroll arm is a sure sign of a recovering project that has been well done. By following the techniques described in this book, even a novice upholsterer can achieve results that look professional.

*Page 1.* Fitted cushions are the most noticeable sections on a piece of upholstery. When cutting out the fabric, make sure that the patterns are centered and that design elements match. (See page 20.)

*Page 3.* With the outer cover removed you will be able to see what repairs need to be made and how you will attach the new cover.

*Back cover*
*Upper left:* A piece of plywood, some batting, and an attractive cover can be turned into an attractive headboard. See page 77 for more details.
*Upper right:* Coordinate the entire bed by upholstering the base to match the cover. See page 79 for covering a bed base and 76 for a fitted bed cover.
*Lower left:* A strip of fabric acts as chair rail molding on upholstered walls. See page 86 for more information on how to upholster walls.
*Lower right:* Throw pillows in different sizes, colors, and patterns liven up a plain-colored sofa. The chapter on cushion- and pillow-making techniques begins on page 65.

# UPHOLSTERING & RECOVERING

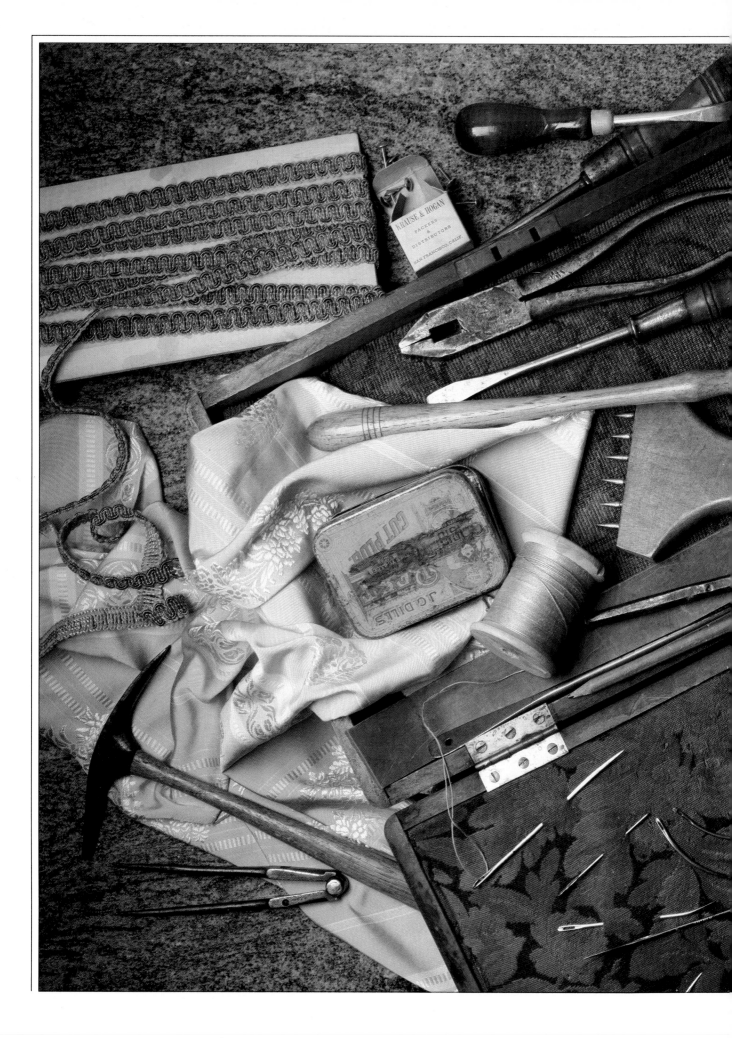

# GETTING READY

T his book, written with the beginner in mind, provides all the information you will need to achieve terrific results in any upholstery project, even if you have never reupholstered anything before.

The methods that are described are for a basic sofa or chair, but you can apply them to almost any type of furniture.

What you find inside your sofa or chair will vary according to how old the piece is and who the manufacturer was, but the inner workings are all based on similar principles and materials.

*Upholstered furniture has been around for a long time, and so have upholsterers as can be evidenced by this antique tool kit. However, you don't have to be as authentically equipped in order to do a professional job. A few simple tools and supplies are all that is required.*

*Above:* The advantage of doing your own upholstering is that you can really coordinate a room. Note how the screen and the throw pillows on the sofa take their cue from the fabric covering the chair.

*Right:* Seat inserts are a good project for a novice upholsterer. They only require a little time and a small amount of fabric for a big change in appearance. (See page 85 for tips on how to upholster seat inserts.)

# AN OVERVIEW

Like many homes, yours may boast a soft old armchair or sofa that seems to have grown more comfortable with the years, even as its upholstery became worn and tattered.

Such furniture is hard to give up, but tossing a blanket over it when company comes only works for so long. You can invest a substantial amount by buying a new piece or having it professionally reupholstered. Or you can take on the project yourself, following the techniques described in this book. When doing the work yourself, the investment is small: A little studying to learn how your piece is constructed, the cost of materials and a few simple tools, and the time and patience to follow a clear-cut series of steps. Your reward will be many more years of comfort from a favorite piece.

## Covering Old Pieces
Whether it's a family fixture that needs renovating or a threadbare flea-market purchase that needs a major overhaul, you are right to consider reupholstery. Old furniture is usually worth reconditioning, sometimes merely for its sentimental value but just as frequently for the intrinsic value of the piece. If it was built to last (and older furniture usually was) then it's worth the effort to reupholster.

## Testing the Quality
You can often tell how sturdily a piece is made simply by the feel as you sit in it, shifting your weight. Wiggle the arms and the back; if they are loose you should do some reinforcing before recovering.

The actual weight of the piece can also give you a clue. Furniture made from heavier woods such as mahogany and oak is more durable. Nowadays the price of good wood is so high that much of the contemporary furniture is made from plywood, particleboard, and veneers. Purchasing a new piece made of fine, solid wood can be very expensive.

On the other hand, if the piece is held together by staples and metal braces rather than dowels, wood braces, and screws, it is probably not worth the effort to rejuvenate it.

## Assessing the Job
Upholstery refers to the fabric, padding, and springs that together make a soft covering for a piece of furniture. As this book explains, you can stretch this basic definition to a variety of less traditional applications. Your project can be simple or complicated. A chair or sofa with straight lines is easier to recover than one with curves. A small piece will probably be quicker to strip and recover than a large one, and it will certainly cost less to buy the fabric needed.

Sometimes the interior of the chair will be in such good shape that you need only replace the outer fabric. At other times you will have to replace or repair parts of the interior.

To assess how big a job lies ahead, lift up the cushion and run your hand over the fabric covering the springs. If the surface is uneven, the springs probably need work. An unpleasant odor may mean that the stuffing needs to be replaced.

Look underneath as well; pull loose a corner of the fabric covering the bottom (called a dust catcher) and inspect the webbing, the crisscrossed strapping that holds the springs in place. If it is sagging or seems badly worn, it will need to be tightened, reinforced, or replaced.

These are all simple repairs, well within the ability of a determined do-it-yourselfer. The techniques are described in detail in this book.

## Decorating Considerations
Once you've decided that a piece is worth reupholstering and that you want to take on the job yourself, think ahead to what decorative role you'd like the particular chair or sofa to perform. Do you need a showpiece— something to arrange all the other objects in the room around? Do you need a unifying element—something to unify nearby patterns with the color and feel of the curtains and carpet? Or do you want it to provide a colorful accent to liven up a monochromatic scheme?

The fact is that a newly covered piece of furniture can change the look and feeling of the whole room as well as the piece of furniture itself.

Color, weight, and texture of the new fabric are all-important. Select a fabric that works in the room in general as well as being suitable for the style of the particular piece.

Also, some fabrics are much easier to work with than others. You may love the look and feel of velvet, but if you're a beginner it is recommended that you avoid this fabric—at least for a large piece of furniture. (Velvet tends to be heavy and, if pieces are cut with the nap going in different directions, the pieces will appear to be different colors.) Particular considerations to bear in mind when choosing a fabric are discussed later in this section.

## Work Place
Reupholstering can be slow work and, if it's your first project, you won't want to be rushèd. You'll need time to become familiar with the "skin and bones" of the furniture; to measure, cut, and sew with precision; and to strip the old cover and replace it with care. Reupholstering is dusty work, and there are a lot of bits and pieces to keep track of. Find a place where you can set up your project and leave it for some time—maybe even weeks

*When choosing fabric, make sure that it will be suitable for the piece itself as well as for the room in which it will be displayed.*

if it's a complicated job and you can only work on it now and then.

In addition, the space needs to be large enough for you to walk around the piece as you work. By elevating the piece, you will avoid having to stoop down all the time or having to work on your knees. Small items can be placed on a tabletop. Larger pieces such as heavy armchairs or sofas are more secure on upholster-er's horses (see pages 18 and 19).

## Stages of Upholstery

The actual recovering of a piece of furniture comes at the end of several preparatory tasks; how many depends on the condition of the piece.

First you should measure the piece with the old cover still in place. (Realize that you must allow enough extra fabric for each piece so it can be fastened to the frame.) This is the time to study the different parts closely and note how they all fit together.

When you start stripping the piece, do so carefully in order to keep the discarded sections of fabric as intact as possible. These old pieces, carefully labeled, will serve as a map as you add the new.

After measuring all parts of the chair or sofa, you will transfer the dimensions to a layout sheet. In this way you'll make the most efficient use of your fabric.

When you strip off the cover, you'll be able to see how much work needs to be done. You may be able to start right in attaching the new cover. On the other hand, repairs may be needed. Springs and webbing may have to be replaced or, more likely, reinforced; padding may have to be replenished; and the frame itself may require strengthening if any of the joints have worked loose. Taking the time to assure the structural integrity is part of assuring the continued usefulness of a piece.

Before fitting on new sections of fabric you might consider adding sheets of batting. These will provide an added layer of comfort and a smooth contour.

# DETAILS

**W**hatever piece of furniture you are covering it will be the details that tell the story. These finishing touches are the most obvious difference between a professional-looking piece of upholstery and an amateurish cover.

This does not mean that chairs and sofas must be trimmed with fringes, rosettes, and welt. But it does mean that corners should lie flat and seams should be straight. Patterned fabrics should be cut so that the design flows from cushion to cushion rather than looking as if a piece were missing.

If your first attempts at making welt do not turn out well, take the extra time and effort to try again or discard the idea of adding welting. However neatly you cover the furniture, badly made or badly applied trim is going to be instantly noticeable and ruin the overall effect.

Most stores that specialize in sewing and upholstery supplies carry a variety of trim. You can get braid hung with pompoms, fringe in many different lengths, tape in solid colors with straight or scalloped edges, ribbon, pleated ribbon, and much more.

If your first upholstery job will be a padded chair seat, you might want to look for decorative, upholstery tacks. These look like larger, stronger thumb tacks. The heads are available in several different finishes.

Be inventive when thinking about trim for your piece. After all, the main reason for doing your own upholstery is to end up with unique furniture that suits the space it occupies.

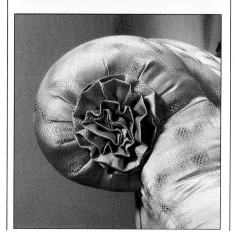

*Make sure that the finishing touches are executed with care. Shaping a cushion, fringing a hem, folding a corner, or adding a rosette are details on which your project will be judged.*

# FABRICS

*I*t goes without saying that your choice of fabric is a very important part of any new covering that you plan to do. Not only does it have to be compatible with fabrics that already exist in the room, but it should also suit the style of the piece you are covering.

If you have, or plan to have, printed fabrics in the room, decide whether you want to introduce yet another one or whether it would be better to use something plain and simple. Don't think that choosing a solid color means you have to give up visual interest, however; many fabrics are available with small designs in the weave. These fabrics have the additional advantage of being less likely to show dirt than a tightly woven solid such as cotton duck.

When choosing fabric for an upholstery project, keep in mind that if you are recovering something as large as a sofa, you are going to see a lot of both the color and the pattern. It is sometimes difficult to judge the effect from a small sample. If possible, bring home swatch books containing fabrics you are considering, or purchase a yard of the fabric, place it on your furniture, and live with it for a few days. It is very important to see how the fabric looks in the light at different times of day, as well as at night with more subdued lighting. Realize the lighting in most fabric stores is quite different from that in your own home.

## Color

If you wish the piece you are working on to be the main focus in a room, you can be a bit adventurous with the fabric selection. Bold stripes and dark colors will make a piece of furniture appear larger.

If you decide upon a solid color but feel that it may not be interesting enough, consider doing the welt in a second color that blends well.

Pastels are timeless and are very easy to live with over a long period of time. You can put together endless combinations when using this area of color. Starting with a soft gray or taupe, you can introduce the shell colors: soft pinks, peach, and apricot. You can also move into the cooler colors such as soft greens, lavender, and gray-blue tones. This color spectrum will lighten a room, will provide an airy feeling if used in a small space, and, depending on the pattern, will work well with many styles of furniture.

If your present scheme is earth-tone colors and you want to introduce something to freshen the overall look without changing the whole room, try using blues—from a bright electric blue to a more muted indigo. To lighten earth tones, try soft shades of gray. If you wish to carry on the theme of earth tones, many of the sand colors will add warmth and tone but will give a lighter feeling.

The bright primary colors, wonderful in children's rooms or in a stark room with contemporary furniture, are easy to match as long as they are true primary colors. Mixing and matching fabrics in this spectrum can be a lot of fun.

For more guidelines on working with color, the chart on page 12 should prove useful.

## Scale

The key to successful mixing of fabrics lies in considering both the scale and the blending of colors. If you decide to mix prints, try to choose fabrics with a blend of colors that is as close as possible to the colors of the existing prints. When trying to match colors, take along a throw cushion, an arm cover, or threads cut from an area that doesn't show.

Scale is important when mixing patterns. If you have already used a lot of small prints and feel that the room is large enough to carry it off, a larger print can work well. On the other hand, if the scheme already includes large-scale prints, try turning to something much smaller. Soft, irregular stripes or small geometrics team wonderfully with floral prints.

## Weight

After color and pattern, weight is another important consideration. Bear in mind that you are going to have to sew through several thicknesses of fabric at a time. Welt, if used, will add even more bulk to the seams. Latex-backed woven fabrics are not recommended because sewing through several layers can really put a strain on both you and your sewing machine. Many medium-weight woven fabrics are loose enough for a needle to penetrate easily. To test this out, take a small sample, fold it into quarters, and run it through your machine to see how it handles the thickness. When choosing a woven fabric, be sure it does not stretch.

At the other extreme, it is not wise to choose a fabric that is too lightweight. The density of the weave in a fabric is known as thread count, usually expressed in threads per inch. This determines its durability; the higher the thread count, the more long-wearing the fabric. If you cannot see a lot of grain in a cotton, it means that the thread count in the fabric is high, and it will therefore last longer.

The front edge and arms of any chair or sofa get the most wear, and these are the areas that will go first if you do not purchase a suitable fabric.

*Before rushing out to purchase the fabric with which to recover a piece, read through the following pages to make sure that your choice is a suitable one.*

# Coordinating Chart

This chart should help you to achieve a cohesive and coordinated look. In case you decide to make some or all of the projects described on pages 76 to 93, the headings in this chart refer to good fabric combinations in a bedroom. However, the same design principles can be applied in any other room in your house. For example, by mentally changing the heading Box Spring to Sofa Frame, Bed Cover to Fitted Cushions, and Headboard to Side Chair, you can plan a design for your living room.

| | *Box Spring* | *Bed Cover* | *Headboard* | *Pillows* |
|---|---|---|---|---|
| *Classic—monochromatic, neutral* | Gray flannel | Same | Same | Soft pastels, either solid fabrics or piping; or grays, taupes with optional piping in black, burgundy, or navy |
| | Unbleached canvas or cotton duck | Same | Same | Same, with matching piping and ruffles, in many different sizes |
| | Plain khaki or tan cotton | Denim | Same as box spring | Madras plaids or school stripes |
| *Country—mixed prints, florals, ethnic prints* | Small pastel floral | Large pastel floral | Small pastel floral | Pillows of assorted sizes in a mix of both fabrics, plus solid colors from both; ruffles or contrasting piping |
| | Plain terra-cotta or blue-gray | French provincial print of earth tones or French blues | Plain fabric to match box spring | Assorted provincial prints, piped in terra-cotta or blue-gray, or bordered in a coordinating print |
| | Textured linen or wool in tan, taupe, or gray | Stripe of taupe and black, or gray and tan | Textured linen or wool to complement box spring, but not the same | Bold African or Guatemalan print |
| | Large floral chintz, warm yellow or bright blue | Same as box spring | Small floral or striped chintz to coordinate | Mixture of both fabrics in ruffled, flanged, and smaller pillows |
| *Contemporary—primary colors, high contrast* | Solid fabric, primary blue | Solid fabric, primary yellow | Solid fabric, primary red | Secondary colors of solid fabrics: orange, purple, green, piped in primaries |
| | Plain black | Black and white stripe, plaid, or zebra pattern | Plain black | Black and white stripes, plaids, polka dots, floral prints, zebra—as varied as possible |
| | Abstract of primary colors or abstract of multiple pastels | Same | Same | Same |
| | Soft butter-yellow | Soft yellow and dove-gray stripe, plaid, or floral | Same as bed cover | Combination of plain fabrics with dove gray and yellow piped in the print |

## Fabric Buying Tips

Along with considerations of color, pattern, texture, weight, and coordination, there are other decisions to be made when choosing a fabric. If this is the first time you have recovered a piece of furniture, your work will be much easier if you pick a solid-colored or small-print fabric that requires little matching.

### Finishes

Many of the 54-inch-wide decorating fabrics have been preshrunk and have been treated with a stain-resistant finish. This finish does not mean that the fabric will not stain at all, only that it will resist stains, especially if any spills are blotted up quickly.

If your fabric is not treated, you can spray a stain-resistant finish onto a piece of furniture once it has been covered. The finish creates a silicone coating that will help resist soil. Apply several coats, following the instructions on the can. It is always a good idea to test a scrap of fabric before spraying the whole piece of furniture. Generally there is no problem, but some fibers or pale-colored fabrics may yellow slightly, and it is better to find this out before you spray.

### Problem Fabrics

When estimating the amount of fabric needed, you must allow extra for a fabric with a definite repeat or a large design that has to be centered, due to the waste involved in matching the design. If you have your heart set on a large repeat, select the fabric before attempting to estimate your yardage, so that you know beforehand exactly how big the repeat is. On some of the larger sections of your piece of furniture, you may end up cutting into a new repeat, meaning that you will have to move to the beginning of the next repeat before cutting the next section. The resulting remnants may be used for smaller parts of the cover that do not need matching. The size of a repeat varies enormously—it can be anywhere from 18 inches to 36 inches or more on a 54-inch-wide fabric.

The other factor to consider is how the design is printed. Sometimes the pattern has to be matched at the selvage, sometimes in the middle, and there can also be a drop repeat (a repeat printed on the diagonal). Read through the Measuring section beginning on page 20 and make a layout marking on it where the repeats fall. From this, work out how to match sections and how much yardage you will need. This is explained in more detail on page 20.

If you are a beginner, avoid strong stripes running across the width. Stripes have to be centered and lined up very carefully. When sewing and tacking, keeping a very strong stripe straight can be a real challenge. For more on this subject, see page 20.

Velvet is another fabric that can cause problems for a novice. It has to be cut so that the nap always runs in the same direction (down the furniture). When you are cutting two pieces together, such as the top and bottom of a cushion with a matched shape, be sure that the velvet is placed with the wrong sides together. If you cut with the two naps together, no matter how tightly pinned the sections are, they will shift and you will not get two accurate cuts.

### Estimating Yardage

Depending on the type of fabric you are using, there are two ways to estimate and cut yardage. The first applies to fabric in which the pattern runs across the width. With this type of fabric, you have to piece longer sections such as the lip, border, skirt, and backs. The second method, called railroading, is applicable to plain fabrics, abstract designs, or to those rare instances when the design runs along the length of the fabric. In such cases, you can cut out your longer lengths in one piece.

If you purchase fabric on sale, be sure that the yardage is all in one piece, and check the entire length for flaws. Working around flaws can increase the amount of yardage needed and will make cutting more difficult. Also be sure to measure carefully so that you purchase enough fabric at one time. Different dye lots can look very different.

## Fabric Types

Below are explanations of some terms used to describe fabrics. You may find some of these printed along the selvage edge.

The chart on pages 14 and 15 describing various fabrics also indicates whether stain removal is difficult or easy. This usually depends on the fiber content. Be sure of the fiber content of your fabric and follow the appropriate cleaning instructions. Scrap pieces from your job can be used for testing soil removers.

*Colorfast.* Fabric that has been treated against fading. Most fabrics, even if they are treated, will fade somewhat over time. This is especially true of darker colors.

*Crease resistant.* Fabric that resists wrinkles. This is generally true of synthetic blends.

*Permanent finish.* Fabric that has been treated in some way to improve the surface (as in a glazed fabric), the general feel of the fabric, or its durability when laundered.

*Preshrunk.* Fabric that has been treated during its manufacture so that there is minimum shrinkage. On a cotton fabric you usually can still expect 2 to 3 percent shrinkage.

*Scotchgard.* A trademark for a stain-resistant finish. This finish will wear off with time and will wash out after several launderings.

*Vat-dyed.* A method of dyeing with insoluble vat colors, which are considered the most resistant to fading caused by cleaning or exposure to sun. The amount of fading will still depend a great deal on the fiber content and the depth of the colors.

# Fabric Types

| Fabric | Fiber Content | Stain Removal | Relative Cost | General Comments |
|---|---|---|---|---|
| **Brocade** A jacquard with a raised design. May be all one color with contrasting surfaces or may have a blend of colors in the weave. This is a very textural fabric. | Silk, satin, or synthetic blends | Silk or satin: difficult; synthetic blends: easier | Medium to high | Good brocades can be expensive and, depending on the fiber content, difficult to work with. Recommended, but use with caution. |
| **Canvas** A stiff, heavy, firmly woven fabric. Generally used for heavy-duty work or for industrial purposes. | Almost always cotton, but sometimes a synthetic blend | Easy except for darker colors, which may fade | Low to medium | Due to the stiffness of this fabric, it is best not to add welt to your cover. The thickness makes it difficult to handle. Otherwise this fabric is highly recommended. |
| **Chenille** The upholstery version of chenille has a fuzzy, close pile that bears a slight resemblance to velvet. | Cotton or synthetic blends | Depending on the fiber content, care must be taken | Medium to high | This is a durable and long-lasting fabric, but its use is not recommended due to the difficulty of working with the nap. |
| **Chintz** A highly glazed fabric that was originally printed in rich floral designs. It now comes in everything from solids to prints. | Cotton | The glaze may come off. Extreme care should be taken | Low to high | In the less expensive varieties, the glaze is strictly on the surface on the fabric. In more expensive fabric, it is rubbed deeper into the fibers and will last longer. The glaze may wear off or launder out. The colors are intense and the fabric easy to work with. Recommended. |
| **Corduroy** A cut-pile fabric with a nap. Available in a wide range of weights, from very light to heavy, depending on the width of the wales. | Cotton or synthetic blends | Not difficult; this is a durable fabric | Low to medium | Due to the difficulty of working with stripes and a nap, this fabric is not recommended. |
| **Duck** Sometimes confused with canvas, duck is lighter in weight and is not as stiff or heavy as canvas. | Generally cotton colors may fade | Easy, but the fabric may shrink and darken | Low to medium | Duck is a crisp, durable fabric that is available in solids and prints. It has become very popular in interior decorating. Highly recommended. |

# Fabric Types (continued)

| Fabric | Fiber Content | Stain Removal | Relative Cost | General Comments |
|--------|---------------|---------------|---------------|------------------|
| **Flannel** A plain, medium-weight fabric with a slight, soft nap to the surface. | Generally wool, but also can be found in a wool-and-synthetic blend | Synthetic blend: easy; wool: more difficult | High | A soft, easy-to-handle fabric, flannel is crease resistant but, depending on the quality, may stretch. It has become popular for upholstery and covering walls. Recommended. |
| **Glazed Cotton** A fabric similar to chintz, glazed cotton has a highly polished surface. | Cotton | Difficult because the glaze will come off | Low to medium | The glaze may wash off and the fabric may shrink unless labeled preshrunk. It will crease, but is recommended if medium- to heavyweight and good quality. |
| **Moire** A rich, shiny fabric that looks like rippling water. This effect is created using special rollers during the manufacturing process with various techniques ranging from pressure and steam to chemicals. | Silk or synthetic blends | Difficult | High | Moire is a sophisticated and classically beautiful fabric, but it is difficult to handle. Not recommended. |
| **Polyester** A general term for synthetic fabric. | Various synthetics | Generally easy | Low to medium | Easy to care for, durable, and crease resistant. It is often blended with natural fibers. Synthetics may run if a thread is pulled or split with a tack or a bad sewing-machine needle. Recommended. |
| **Twill** Although there are several variations, twill generally has a diagonal rib running through the weave. Available in medium to heavy weights. | Cotton, wool, or synthetic blends | Care should be taken; check the fiber content | Medium to high | This fabric is not recommended due to the difficulty of working with a diagonal, ribbed weave. |
| **Velvet** This fabric is soft and luxurious to the touch, with a short, dense pile. | Cotton or rayon | Extremely difficult | Medium to high | Very difficult to work with, velvet must be cut carefully, with the nap going in the correct direction. Not recommended. |

# MATERIALS

The decorative fabric for your new outer cover is very important. See pages 14 and 15 if you need help in deciding what type of fabric to use. In addition, you will need fabric for the decking, which is the part of the seat on which the seat cushions rest, and for the dust catcher, which covers the outside of the piece.

## Interior Fabrics

You can use any sturdy, plain fabric for the decking as well as for the stretchers, which are pieces sewn on to your cover to add length in hidden places. Stretchers are used to economize on yardage. Other kinds of fabrics used in invisible places on the furniture follow.

### Cambric

This is a gauzy black fabric typically used as a dust catcher underneath a piece of furniture.

### Burlap

A coarsely woven fabric made of jute, burlap is used to cover the springs and webbing. It is also tacked onto the rails and covers the inside seat, back, and arms, creating a smooth surface and form for later padding and recovering.

## Basic Upholstery Materials

You will need at least some of the following materials for any project you undertake. Sources include professional upholsterers' shops and many fabric stores.

### Webbing

Webbing is used on the bottom of furniture and in some cases on the arms and backs. If the webbing has rotted and you are unable to re-stretch it, it must be replaced. For most jobs 3½-inch-wide webbing is recommended.

### Tacking Strips

These ½-inch-wide cardboard strips are used for blind-tacking. Tacking strips keep the edges of the fabric flat and straight on surfaces such as outer arms and skirts. You can either purchase tacking strips or you can cut them yourself, being careful to keep the edges very straight.

### Edge Roll or Fox Edging

An edge roll is a burlap tube filled with one of a variety of padding materials. It is tacked or sewn to the edge of the frame to protect the outer cover from wear and also to keep the seat cushions in place. Another use is for softening hard edges. Jute-filled edge roll is recommended.

### Cotton Padding

The padding lies directly underneath the finished cover. It is approximately 1 inch thick, is sold by the yard, and can be cut to size. Although it stays together in a matted form, cotton padding should be handled carefully while working as it does pull apart. Even if you are reusing your old padding, it is a good idea to add an additional layer of new padding so that your cover fabric rests on a clean surface.

### Polyester Batting

Batting is used to wrap seat and back cushions before they are covered. While not necessary, wrapping cushions in batting gives them a softer look that many find more appealing than the sharp corners of unwrapped foam cushions. For most upholstery projects, the best batting is the type that is covered on one side with a light synthetic material that keeps the batting in place. You can also buy batting that is uncovered or that is covered on both sides.

### Foam

Examine any foam that you find used as padding on the arms, seat, or back cushions. It should still have bounce and should not be crumbly. If the foam has to be replaced, purchase the same thickness as the old foam. Take your measurements from the parts you are replacing.

### Welt Cord

Jute welt cord is made from the same fiber as burlap and is the choice of many upholsterers. Other varieties are available, but jute is the most flexible to work with. Welt cord is covered with fabric and sewn into the seams along the outer edges of the finished cover. Use ³⁄₃₂-inch welt cord for most jobs.

### Gimp

More commonly known as braid, gimp is used to cover tacks and seams on the outer edges of some styles of furniture. Although not normally used on contemporary furniture, it was very popular in Victorian times, and there currently seems to be a revival in its use.

### Spring Twine

This is a strong waxed twine used for retying springs.

### Thread

You will need two different types of thread. Use a heavy-duty sewing thread for the main cover, cushions, and nylon tufting. Use button twine to sew the springs to the webbing as well as to sew the edge roll and the burlap to the springs.

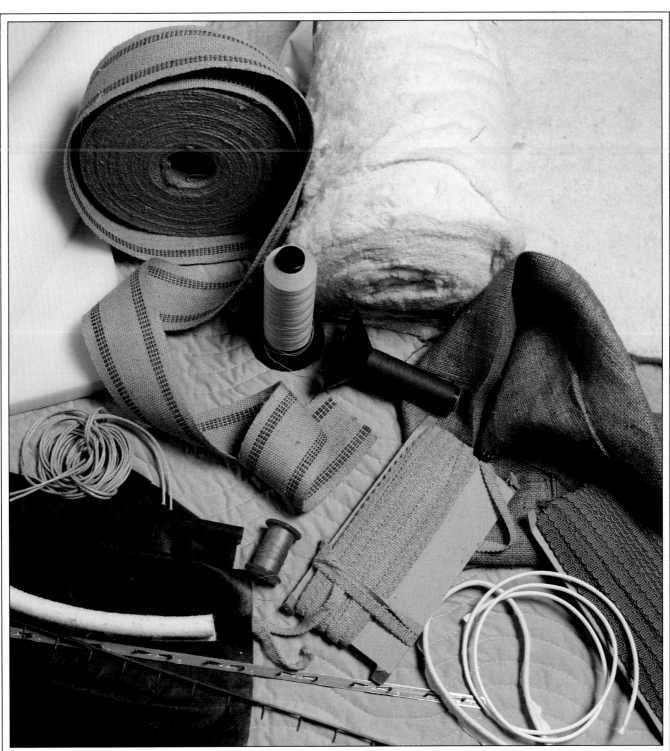

*Most of the materials and supplies needed for upholstering can be found at a good sewing-supply store. If you have difficulty finding a particular item, check your Yellow Pages for upholstery suppliers in your area.*

# TOOLS & SUPPLIES

Following is a list of the tools and supplies needed for the projects in this book. Having the right equipment on hand will make your projects much faster and easier to complete.

Take a close look at your particular piece of furniture before you rush out to buy each item. You may not need all these tools for the project. Of the tools that you need, you may already own some, and you may find that you can substitute tools you already own for ones on the list. Other tools you may be able to make yourself.

The items you decide to purchase can be found in hardware stores, home center stores, and stores selling fabrics and supplies for home decorating, or they can be obtained from an upholstery supplier.

## Shears
Good, sharp sewing shears with a 5- or 6-inch blade will be suitable for most fabrics.

## Utility Knife
A knife with a replaceable or retractable blade is very useful for cutting away fabric or twine in areas difficult to reach with shears. You can substitute a small, sharp kitchen knife.

## Knife
A finely serrated bread knife or an electric carving knife works well for cutting foam. You can also use a hacksaw with a fine blade.

## Staple Remover
This tool facilitates removing staples, even if they are buried in the wood.

## Claw Tool
Useful for removing staples and tacks, this tool also makes it easier to remove old fabric from tight areas.

## Tack Hammer
The magnetized end of a tack-hammer head picks up and holds tacks, making accurate placement easier. Tacks can be driven partway in with the magnetized end, then pounded down with the opposite end. You can substitute a regular hammer.

## Tacks
The size of the tacks you need will vary according to the job, but the sizes most commonly used for the projects in this book are number 2 and number 3 for tacking fabric, number 10 for tacking webbing and for blind-tacking cardboard, and number 16 for tying springs. The lower the number, the finer the tack.

## Webbing Stretcher
You need this tool only if the webbing is sagging or has rotted and needs to be replaced. Two kinds of stretchers are available: one has a curved handle and the other has a solid wooden handle. The latter type is more commonly used and is recommended as the more efficient tool.

Should you have trouble finding this tool, it is not difficult to fabricate one using a piece of wood 6 to 7 inches long and 3½ inches wide with nails driven into it.

## Webbing Pliers
These pliers grip the webbing while you pull on it. They can also be used for the same purpose as the spiked webbing stretcher.

## Pliers
These are a must. Regular household pliers will work well. They will help you to rip off the old fabric and pull out stubborn staples, tacks, and nails.

## Staple Gun
Although you may find a staple gun useful at times, it is strongly recommended that you use tacks and a hammer for most of the work.

If you choose to use a staple gun, use one that you can operate with one hand, leaving the other hand free to hold the fabric firmly in place.

## Upholsterer's Horses
These stands are used by professional upholsterers to make working on a piece of furniture easier. The piece is elevated and it is easy to reach all of the parts to be worked on.

Upholsterer's horses can be made by purchasing regular sawhorses and adding a padded trough. Or you can use an old picnic table or stand covered with fabric to protect your new coverings.

## Needles
Stock up on upholstery needles. You will need a 10-inch needle with a triangular point on both ends for sewing the springs to the webbing and for attaching buttons and the edge roll. Use a 3-inch curved needle with a round point for hand-sewing the outsides. A 6-inch, curved triangular-pointed needle will be handy for sewing burlap to springs and attaching stuffing to burlap, and will have many other uses as well.

## Pins
T-form pins, or skewers, are used as a temporary basting for the covers.

## Yardstick
A yardstick is helpful when you need a straight edge.

## Chalk
You will need chalk for marking fabric. The sort of chalk used on a slate blackboard is recommended, as it marks well and is easily brushed off the fabric.

## Tape Measure
For measuring furniture and fabric, a metal tape measure is easier to work with than a cloth one.

## Sewing Machine
A sewing machine is essential for many aspects of upholstery work. Have on hand a supply of needles suitable for the weight of fabric you will be using, and make sure that you have a zipper foot for sewing in zippers and for making welt.

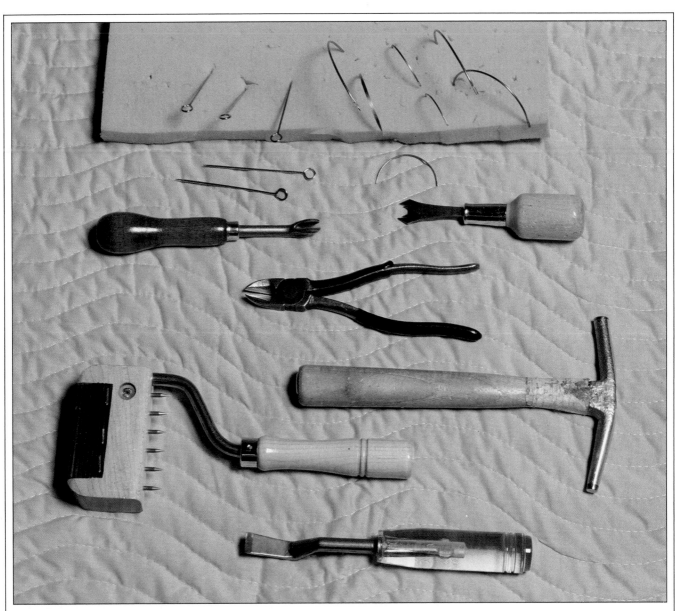

**Above:** *With these tools you will be able to tackle any upholstery project. Your workshop should contain most of them with the possible exception of a webbing stretcher.*

**Left:** *Upholsterer's horses are what professionals use to elevate a piece so it can be worked on easily. Space horses so that furniture legs sit squarely in the padded troughs.*

# MEASURING

The following information will help you estimate how much fabric you will need for your new cover. All the measuring and cutting instructions in this section are based on 54-inch-wide fabric. Most upholstery fabrics are 54 inches wide and this is the most economical width to work with. If you do some careful planning, only a little fabric need be wasted.

## Drawing a Layout

Figuring out the layout on paper first will save a lot of time, effort, and wasted yardage.

To make a paper layout, use graph paper and a scale that suits your purposes. For example, if your fabric is 54 inches wide and you want one square to equal one inch, the paper must have at least 54 squares across the width of one sheet. Use the same scale for the amount of yardage, that is 36 squares equals one yard. This will probably require taping several pieces of paper together.

Reduce your pattern pieces to the same scale and cut them out of paper. Then you can arrange and rearrange the paper pieces to find the most economical cutting layout and to ascertain the amount of fabric you need to buy.

Maybe you already have the fabric, or maybe you can tell that you will need practically the entire width for most pieces, or maybe you have chosen inexpensive fabric. In any of these cases, it will be simpler to do the layout directly on the fabric using actual pattern pieces. Choose a working surface that is flat and hard, smooth out the entire fabric length, and lay the patterns in place.

Before pinning the patterns in place and cutting them out, be sure to read through the two sections that follow: Laying out the Pieces and Cutting the Pieces. These sections contain tips and advice, including how much fabric you should allow for attaching pieces to the frame.

## Laying out Fabric

If you are using a plain fabric or one with a small print that does not require any matching, layout will be straightforward and you can concentrate on placing pieces in such a way as to require the least amount of yardage.

### Railroading

Some patterns allow the fabric to be railroaded, meaning that the design works when lengths of fabric are spread across the width of the piece to be covered. Railroading generally results in using less fabric. However, realize that this cutting method may not be suitable for your project because no single piece can be longer than the width of the fabric.

### Direction of Weave

If you are using velvet or any fabric with a heavy grain, a deep pile, or a large pattern, be sure to mark the direction in which the piece of fabric will be placed on the paper pattern. If pieces are cut in different directions, the finished cover will look patchy and very amateurish.

## Centering and Matching Designs

If the fabric you are using has a large repeat that has to be matched and centered, you should plan for this when doing the layout. Bear in mind that the design should be centered over both the top and underside of seat cushions (so that you can turn them over), the inside back, outside back, inside arms, outside arms, lip, border, and skirt.

To make sure that a pattern element will be centered on the pieces mentioned above, proceed as follows. First pick the element that you would like to center. On the fabric, find the repeat and measure the distance between. Also measure the distance between the edge of the fabric and the first occurrence of your chosen element. Translate these measurements into the scale chosen for your paper layout.

On the graph paper, measure from the line indicating the edge of the fabric to the spot where the design element first appears, make a mark here. Make marks indicating each repeat then draw lines down the entire piece of paper at these marks. Either mark the center of each paper pattern or fold it in half and use the crease as the mark. Lay out the paper patterns so that the centerline on the pattern matches one of the design-element lines that you marked on the graph paper.

*When working with a fabric that has a large and very dramatic pattern, it is particularly important that individual sections flow together. To achieve a look as handsome as these professionally upholstered pieces, you must take care when laying out, cutting, and attaching separate sections.*

*Rails refer to the pieces of wood that both strengthen the frame and allow you to staple or tack individual sections in place. Once exposed, your frame may not look quite like the ones shown, but it should be easy to figure out which are the top, bottom, and side rails referred to in the recovering directions.*

## Layout Considerations

When measuring the inside back section to determine how to center a design, remember to deduct the depth of the boxing on the seat cushions—this is very important. Center large designs with the cushions in place. By doing this, you will be placing the design toward the top of the inside back rather than right in the middle, but when the seat cushions are in place, the design will appear centered.

If a back cushion will partially cover the seat cushion, you will need to shift the design on the seat cushion off center, toward the front of the cushion, so that it appears centered once both cushions are in place. To do this, deduct the amount of the boxing on the back cushion from the seat-cushion measurement.

If you have chosen a strong stripe that runs across the width of the fabric, carefully mark the center of your piece of furniture on the inside back, choose the stripe that you wish to be centered (this will usually be the predominant stripe), and line it up before you measure and cut. Match the center seat cushion with the back stripe, and then move to the outsides to line up the remaining stripes.

With predominant stripes, the inside back, seat cushions, boxing, and lip can all be matched, but it will be impossible to have the boxing match when the cushions are turned over. With this type of fabric you cannot match everything.

## Laying out the Pieces

The list of furniture sections that follow and the sample measurements on page 26 are based on a sofa with three seat cushions, three back cushions, no border, and a one-piece skirt with a 21-inch allowance for each of the kick pleats. These examples are intended as guides to show how to estimate your yardage and plan a cutting layout. Your sections and measurements will be different.

## Direction of Pattern and Nap

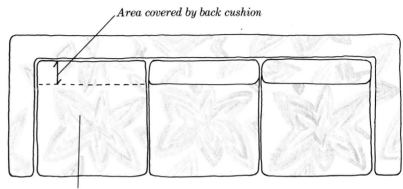

Area covered by back cushion

Center the design to face front of seat cushion

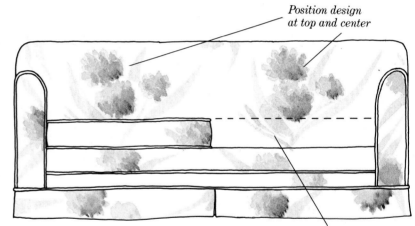

Position design at top and center

Area covered by seat cushion

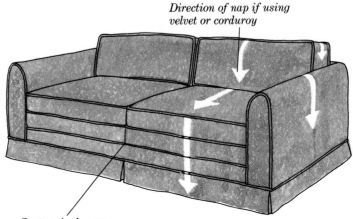

Direction of nap if using velvet or corduroy

Center single seam. If more than one seam, space equally across front

## Measuring the Lip Area

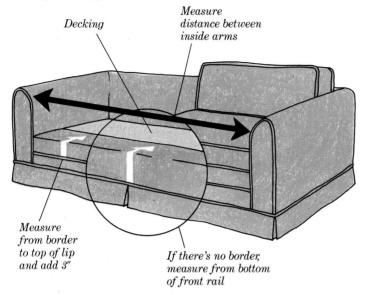

Decking

Measure distance between inside arms

Measure from border to top of lip and add 3"

If there's no border, measure from bottom of front rail

The measurements given here include allowances for seams and tacking. All seams are ½ inch; the tacking allowances will be given separately. The allowances given are generous. If, when you remove your cover, you find that they are not sufficient, you can always add a stretcher. A stretcher is simply a piece of sturdy fabric added to hidden areas for the purpose of increasing the length of the finish fabric.

With the old cover still on, measure the widest point of each section of the piece of furniture from top to bottom and from side to side, as directed in the following sections. Add the allowances for seams and tacking to this measurement (these are given in the instructions for the individual sections below). Copy the list of sections given here, filling in your own measurements, and then draw your layout on graph paper, working to scale. Number the yards along the side of the layout, then draw in each of the sections needed for your chair or sofa. (Remember to include the material needed for welt, if you plan to use it.)

### Lip

If your piece of furniture has no border, measure the lip from the bottom of the front frame. If it has a border, begin measuring at the point where the border and lip meet. Measure up and over the finished edge of the lip to where it meets the decking. Add 3 inches for the seam and tacking allowance. Measure the width from inside arm to inside arm. If the lip is 5 inches deep, add a 10-inch allowance to the width measurement for the corners of the lip. For other lip depths, double the depth measurement and add this figure to the width measurement. For example, with a 4-inch-deep lip, add 4 inches to each side of the width. This is important when there is a centered pattern.

When covering a sofa in velvet or in a pattern that cannot be railroaded, the lip and other long sections will have to be pieced. Measure from the border or frame to the decking, as directed above, but for the width, measure the front of the lip and divide this figure by 3 (for a three-cushion sofa). Add 5 inches (or less, depending on the depth of the lip on your piece of furniture) to each end piece, and add a ½-inch seam allowance to each edge to be pieced. This spaces the seams evenly across the front of the furniture and provides the necessary allowance to pull around the sides of the lip.

When cushion sizes vary, or when covering a two-cushion sofa, place seams where the cushions meet.

### Inside Back

Measure from the seat up and over the back to the bottom of the top back rail. Add 6 inches for seams and tacking. Unless you are railroading your fabric, you will need to piece this section together for a sofa. To space the seams evenly, proceed as follows: Measure from side to side, and add the tacking and seam allowances. Deduct the 54-inch width from this measurement (for your center section). Divide the remainder by 2, and cut two sections this size. These will be sewn to each side of the complete 54-inch-wide piece. If you are matching a pattern, the two side sections must be matched carefully; this may require using the selvage.

If you wish your seams to fall in a specific area, measure and divide the sections accordingly; remember to add seam and tacking allowances.

### Outside Back

Measure from the top back rail to the bottom back rail and add 3 inches. From side to side, add a ½-inch seam allowance on each side. Piece the outside back in the same way as described for the inside back.

### Inside Arm

Measure the inside arm from front to back and add an additional tacking allowance of 6 inches. Measure from the top of the arm to the seat and add 6 inches. If you have a boxed arm without a welt or an inner seam, measure from the seat over the top of the arm to the point where it connects with the outside arm; add 6 inches to this measurement. For a scroll arm, measure from the seat up the inside arm and over the top to the tacking rail where it meets the outside arm section; then add 6 inches.

### Outside Arm

Measure the outside arm from frame top to frame bottom; add 3 inches. Measure across the outside frame edges at the widest point and add a ½-inch seam allowance to each side.

### Seat Cushions

Cut a square 2 inches larger than your finished measurement. Adjustments will be made later. The cushion covers should be made after the inside back and inside arms are completely reupholstered. Once these areas are completed, put the seat cushions in place to see how they fit; make any necessary adjustments by adding or reducing the amount of stuffing. Now add a ½-inch seam allowance on each side; cut your cushion covers to fit exactly.

Occasionally the two side cushions on a sofa are not exactly square; the front edges may curve a little. If this is the case, position the fabric wrong side up and mark the outline with chalk; add a ½-inch seam allowance.

### Boxing for Seat Cushions

Add a couple of extra inches to the depth of the boxing. This will provide enough depth for the sections of boxing that have a zipper. The remaining sections can be cut to size later.

### Back Cushions

Measure the length and width of the back cushions, then add ½-inch seam allowances all around. Or, use your old cushion covers as a pattern.

### Boxing for Back Cushions

Add 2 inches to the depth of the back-cushion boxing to allow for the sections that have a zipper.

### Skirt

The two methods that follow are the most common ways to make a skirt. Either type can be lined with a lining fabric or be self-lined by folding the fabric in half. Self-lining is faster, as it eliminates extra seams.

The first method involves making the skirt in separate sections, with the

### Shirred Skirt

*Allow 2½ times the perimeter measurement*

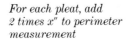

### Spaced Box Pleat

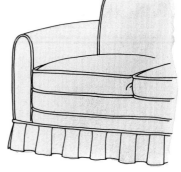

*Allow 2½ times the perimeter measurement*

### Kick Pleat

*For each pleat, add 2 times x″ to perimeter measurement*

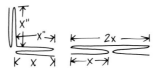

### Joined Box Pleats

*Allow 3 times the perimeter measurement*

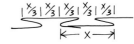

pleats formed by folding the ends of sections of fabric under and tacking them over another section that forms the back of the pleats. The second method is to sew all of the pieces together and fold in the kick pleats.

Measure the old skirt (unless you are making the new skirt in a different style), and proceed as follows:

*Method 1.* For a skirt made in separate pieces with a separate lining, measure the drop of the skirt and add 2 inches. Cut the lining 2 inches shorter than the outer skirt, because 1 inch of the outer fabric will be turned under to form the hem.

To make a self-lined version of the same style of skirt, double the drop measurement and add a ½-inch seam allowance at the top only.

The number of sections and their length will depend on how many pleats you plan to have. When you have decided on the finished length of the sections, add 4½ inches to each end of these sections. (Add 9 inches altogether to each section.) This will give you the seam allowances plus 4 inches to fold under at each side to form the pleats.

The sections that will form the backs of the pleats should be 5 inches wide, and should have the same drop as the main skirt.

*Method 2.* If you are sewing the skirt all in one piece and folding in the kick pleats, measure the circumference of your piece of furniture around the base of the front, back, and sides, and add 21 inches per pleat to this measurement. Measure the drop in the same way as described for the lined or self-lined sectioned skirt.

Plan to conceal any seams in the fold of the pleats. This should be taken into consideration before cutting, especially if you are matching a pattern on the skirt. Instead of placing the seam in the center of the

21-inch allowance, cut the sections different lengths to avoid having a seam in the center of a finished kick pleat.

## Border

Measure from the point where the border meets the lip on the front rail to the bottom front rail; add 3 inches to this measurement. If the border does not extend all the way down the front of the furniture, but instead meets a skirt, measure from this point to the lip and add 2 inches. This gives a seam allowance for the welt, tacking area, and stuffing. If you need to piece the border, follow the instructions for piecing the lip.

## Front Arm Panels

Measure the length of a front arm panel from top to bottom, and measure the width at its widest point. Add 3 inches to each measurement. This will give you the allowance needed to turn under and attach the panel. Or, once they have been cut and removed, use the old covers as a pattern for shaping the new ones, tracing the outline in chalk.

## Wings

For both the inside and outside wings, measure the width and length at the widest points; add 3 inches for tacking. The final shaping should be done on the chair itself later, as you are reupholstering it.

## Decking

Measure the existing decking on the seat area, add ½-inch seam allowances to the front and the back and 6-inch tacking allowances to each side. The decking may be made either from a plain, sturdy fabric, as is generally the case, or from your outer cover fabric if you do not need to economize. If you are recovering a sofa and you make the decking in the same fabric, there is no need to place strips of fabric underneath the seat cushions as suggested on page 53.

## Stretchers

Tacking allowances have been made for the stretchers that pull through the frame and are tacked into the rails. Stretchers can be made separately, however, and sewn to the cover fabric if you need to cut back on the amount of fabric used in your piece. You may use any plain, sturdy fabric as stretchers.

## Sample Measurements

Below is a list of furniture sections with sample measurements. Copy this list and fill it in with your own measurements. This will enable you to calculate your yardage requirements and determine a cutting layout.

Lip: 14″ x 80″

Inside back: 28″ x 90″

Outside back: 30″ x 84″

Inside arm: 26″ x 32″

Outside arm: 17″ x 32″

Seat cushions: 3 @ 25″ x 25″ each

Boxing for seat cushions: 6 pieces @ 6″ x 54″ each

Back cushions: 3 @ 16″ x 25″ each

Boxing for back cushions: 6 pieces @ 6″ x 54″ each

### Common Variations

Border: 15″ x 78″

Skirt: 6 pieces @ 13″ x 54″

Front arm panels (front): 2 @ 5″ x 22″

Wings (outside): 10″ x 16″

Wings (inside): 20″ x 16″

**Note:** The seat- and back-cushion boxing sections include an allowance for the zippered sections. Skirt measurement is based on a self-lined version with a 21-inch allowance per kick pleat.

## Cutting the Pieces

Once you have completed your measuring, estimated yardage, purchased the fabric, and made a cutting layout, you are ready to begin cutting.

Before you start, be sure that the edge of the fabric is straight across the width. To do this, either make a snip through the selvage and pull a thread across, or make a snip and tear a straight edge. Once the tear is made, find a continuous thread and pull it across. Next, carefully recheck all of your measurements. If your furniture needs additional tacking allowances, add stretchers.

If you do not need the selvage edges for matching a pattern or for an additional allowance when fitting your pieces, cut them off. The selvage often causes seams to pucker.

Measure each section on the right side of the fabric, following your layout. Using chalk and a yardstick, mark the cutting lines of the pieces and cut them out.

Make the largest cuts—that is, the horizontal cuts—first. You will need extra fabric to make the piece large enough to cover the inside and outside back, lip, border, and so forth.

Be sure to mark the pieces on the wrong side to identify them. It is also a good idea to mark the top of each piece, especially when working with a patterned fabric. To speed up sewing the sections together, indicate on the label of pieced sections such as the back, border, or lip whether they are left, right, or center.

Welt does not have to be cut on the bias unless you are working with velvet or a napped fabric. If using the edges of your fabric for the welt, first remove the selvage and, using a yardstick, mark 1½-inch strips along the longest pieces you can find. The longer the strips, the fewer seams necessary. For double welt make your cuts 2½ inches wide.

Cutting on the bias gives the welt more flexibility around curves. To cut on the bias, chalk diagonal lines across the fabric, 1¾ inches apart.

*It is easy for fabric to slip and become slightly out of position when it is stretched and attached to the frame. Even though you have done an accurate layout and cut pieces out carefully, it is important to check and recheck as you work. Stripes that do not follow the contours of a piece of upholstered furniture are a sure sign of an amateurish job.*

# SEWING

*T*his section gives instructions for the various sewing tasks you will perform as you reupholster. What is not discussed here is how to sew new covers for cushions; instructions for covering a variety of cushions and pillows are given on pages 65 to 73.

Upholstering does not require a great deal of sewing; most of the work involves fitting the fabric over the frame and either tacking it in place or hand-sewing it. The only supplies you will need are sewing-machine needles (in the correct size for the weight of fabric you are sewing), heavy-duty thread, and a zipper foot. Remember that all seams are ½ inch unless specified differently.

## Welt

It is best to make the welt as you go along, so that you can be sure the seams are hidden at the back of the piece of furniture. In an area such as the inside back, place seams at equal intervals for a more professional look.

To join two strips of fabric, place them at right angles to each other, right sides together, and make a diagonal seam. To eliminate bulk, trim away the excess to approximately ¼ inch and press open the seam.

### Single Welt

Place the cord in the center of the strip, on the wrong side of the fabric. Fold the fabric over so that the edges meet and, using the zipper-foot attachment on your machine, stitch along the length of the fabric, as close to the cord as possible.

When you sew the covered welt cord to the sections of the cover, be

sure that you stitch just inside the line of stitches on the welt (closer to the cord), so that they do not show.

When you begin sewing cord to a section of fabric, leave a couple of inches free, with enough extra fabric for seaming the two ends together. Sew the cord in place on the section of fabric, stopping a couple of inches before the end. Sew the two sections

with a bias seam. Trim the ends of the cord so that they butt together (they should not overlap), position the cord in the welt fabric, and finish stitching it to the piece you are working on.

### Double Welt

Usually on double welt, a 3-inch-wide strip of fabric is cut to the required length. If the pieces are not

## Making Single Welt

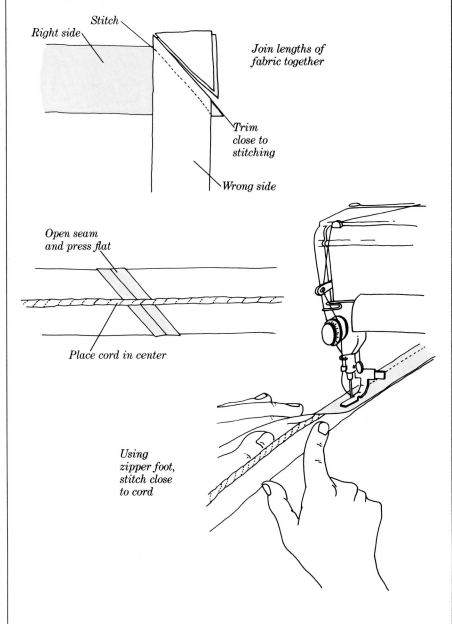

Stitch

Right side

Join lengths of fabric together

Trim close to stitching

Wrong side

Open seam and press flat

Place cord in center

Using zipper foot, stitch close to cord

## Making Double Welt

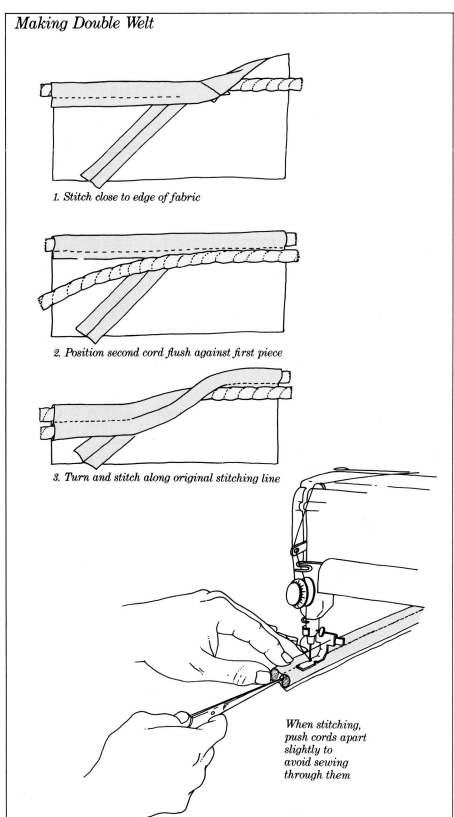

*1. Stitch close to edge of fabric*

*2. Position second cord flush against first piece*

*3. Turn and stitch along original stitching line*

*When stitching, push cords apart slightly to avoid sewing through them*

long enough, they should be seamed together in the same way as with the single welt. With the wrong side of the fabric facing you, wrap just enough of the fabric over the cord to have sufficient excess to stitch along; machine-stitch.

Lay the second cord alongside the finished one. Fold the fabric over so that the raw edge is on the bottom and the two wrapped cords and line of stitching faces you. Place under the sewing-machine foot.

With the tip of your scissors carefully inserted between the two cords, push down the stitching and slightly separate the cords. Sew precisely on top of the first line of stitching. After the second cord is sewn in, turn over the completed double welt and trim away the excess fabric as close to the stitching as possible taking care not to cut it.

Double welt is glued into place. When gluing, start in a back corner of the furniture and make a bias (or mitered) cut at the end of the welt. Apply glue to the back. To hold the welt in place while the glue dries, pin-tack it at approximately 1-foot intervals with number 10 tacks. Insert a blunt instrument such as a screwdriver between the two welts, pinching them together as you work, so that the row of stitching will not show once the glue is dry.

When the glue is completely dry, remove pin tacks with pliers twisting the tacks to break them away from the glue; then pull them straight out.

Once all of the tacks are removed, run over the holes with the tip of the scissors or a screwdriver to push the threads of the fabric back together.

To join the end of the double welt to the beginning, make a bias (or mitered) cut, but in the opposite direction to the cut made at the other end. Be sure to cut the cords slightly shorter than the fabric. Carefully place the mitered corners together, apply a little glue, and press in the small amount of excess fabric to eliminate visible raw edges.

# Skirt

There are two ways to sew a skirt that will be attached to a sofa. (See page 63 for directions on how to attach it.)

## Method 1

Use the first method if you are making the skirt in separate sections. Sew the top sections, which fold under to form the pleats, as follows: Place the outer fabric and lining right sides together, with the hem edges even. Sew along the hem. Shift the outer fabric so that the top edges of the skirt are together, and pin. Sew the sides; remove the pins. Trim the corners and turn the whole piece right side out and press. One inch of your outer fabric will be turned under, forming a hem on the inside of the skirt.

*Self-lined version.* If, instead of using a separate lining fabric, you are making a self-lined version of this style of skirt, fold the fabric in half, right sides together, with the top edges even. Sew the side seams, trim the corners, turn the piece right side out, and press.

Fold under 4 inches at each end and press this into a pleat. Make the underneath pleat sections in the same way as the skirt, omitting the welt at the top. These pieces will be tacked in later.

*Sewing on the welt.* Once you are sure that the pleats are placed correctly, sew the welt for the skirt into a complete circle before attaching it to the skirt. Measure carefully. The seam in the center back where the two ends join should be sewn together on the bias. Leave a small hole in this seam and let enough cord trail through this hole to enable you to make adjustments later.

Sew the welt completely around the skirt, leaving approximately 1½ inches free at each end for making adjustments later when you tack or hand-sew the skirt to the furniture.

If you are making this style of skirt self-lined, fold the fabric, right sides together, with the top edges even. Sew the side seams together, trim corners, turn right side out, and press.

Following the directions for sewing on the welt, treat the underneath pleat sections as you did the skirt but omit the welt.

## Method 2

For a one-piece skirt, in which the pleats are folded into one long strip of fabric, sew all of your sections together after checking that each seam will fall slightly off center inside a pleat so that it does not show.

If you are using a lining, sew the lining sections together and then, with the right sides of the fabric and lining together and the bottom edges even, sew along the hem. Turn right side out and, with the top edges even, press the hem under. One inch of the outer fabric should now be turned under to form a hem.

If you are making a self-lined version of this style of skirt, fold the fabric in half, right sides together, with the edges even at the top. Press the bottom hem.

Measure for accurate placement of the pleats and fold the fabric under on each side so that the center folds of the pleat meet evenly. Make sure that the seams in the skirt are hidden in the side fold of the pleats. Baste and press the pleats.

Sew the welt around the top of the skirt. The inner edge of the cord should be ½ inch below the top edge. Begin sewing at the center back, leaving a couple of inches of the cord unattached and a bit of excess cord for fitting and adjustment, as described for the first method of constructing a skirt.

## Making a Skirt in Separate Sections

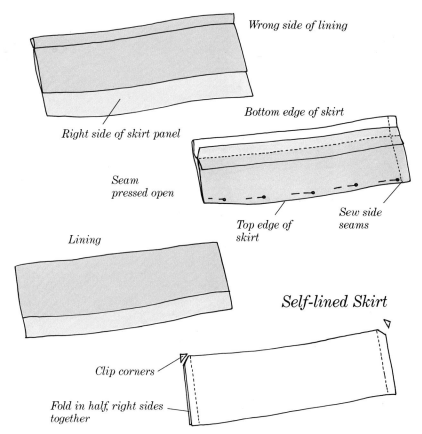

*Wrong side of lining*

*Right side of skirt panel*

*Bottom edge of skirt*

*Seam pressed open*

*Top edge of skirt*

*Sew side seams*

*Lining*

## Self-lined Skirt

*Clip corners*

*Fold in half, right sides together*

## Forming Pleats

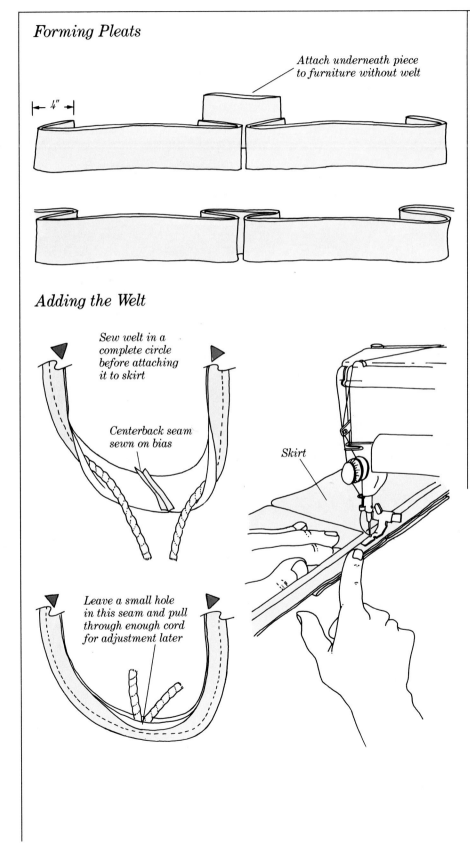

Attach underneath piece to furniture without welt

4"

## Adding the Welt

Sew welt in a complete circle before attaching it to skirt

Centerback seam sewn on bias

Leave a small hole in this seam and pull through enough cord for adjustment later

Skirt

## Deck and Lip

The deck and lip are sewn together and the outer corners of the lip are sewn to form a boxed shape. Since this has to be fitted carefully to the furniture, directions and illustrations for the sewing are given on page 53.

## Fitted Arm Panel

If the furniture has a scroll arm with a fitted front panel sewn to the cover, first make the welt and cut a length that will extend all the way around the outer edge of the front panel.

Beginning at the bottom inside edge of the panel, pin the welt even with the edge on the front of the panel. Fit the cord around the scroll, stopping about 1 inch under the scroll and leaving the rest hanging free. Loose cord will be tacked to the outer edge of the panel later. Pin the inside arm section to the front panel and the welt, right sides together.

Starting at the bottom inside edge of the front panel and ending where the welt stitching stops, sew the pieces together. You will fit the top part of the arm section over the arm and tack it to the outside rail later.

### Fitted Arm Panel

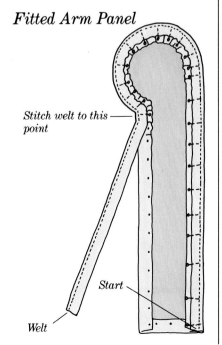

Stitch welt to this point

Start

Welt

# REMOVING THE OLD COVER

Here's the part you've been waiting for—getting rid of that torn and dusty cover. But remember that the old pieces of covering will be invaluable as guides. Curb your enthusiasm and do this carefully and methodically.

Once the cover is removed, it is quite likely that you will find the frame needs a few repairs before you can begin recovering. Simple repairs such as replacing webbing, retying springs, and regluing joints can be done by following the techniques described in this chapter. However, if the piece appears to need extensive surgery you might reevaluate the practicality of rejuvenating it or seek professional help.

*You might think that your torn and tattered upholstered chair could not possibly look worse than it already does. Just wait until you remove the cover! Wear old clothes, heavy-soled shoes, and have a large garbage bag on hand.*

# PREPARATION

**B**efore starting your project, read the following pages carefully. Some of the steps may not apply to your individual piece of furniture.

Becoming familiar with the process before you begin will make you better able to judge whether the webbing in your project needs to be stretched or replaced. You will be able to tell what condition the springs are in, and whether the batting (padding) should be replaced.

The illustration below shows the parts of the piece that will be exposed as you strip sections of fabric away. Although this is a simplified drawing, all fully upholstered chairs and sofas, no matter how complicated or ornate, consist of basically these elements. You can refer to this drawing as you work if you need guidance in following the steps. In any case, if you detach each piece of fabric carefully so that it remains intact, the pieces can later be used as patterns for measuring, cutting, and placing the new cover. To be sure that you can identify the pieces, attach a strip of masking tape to each one and mark on the tape which section it is. Do the same when you remove the burlap. Making mental or written notes regarding where each section was attached before you removed it will give you an overall picture of your project. It will also make it much easier to follow the directions.

As this is the messiest part of the project, be sure to organize your work area so that dust, loose threads, wads of padding, and stray tacks and staples don't get spread around. It is helpful to spread a tarpaulin to define the boundaries of your work space and to make cleaning up easier.

## Anatomy of a Sofa

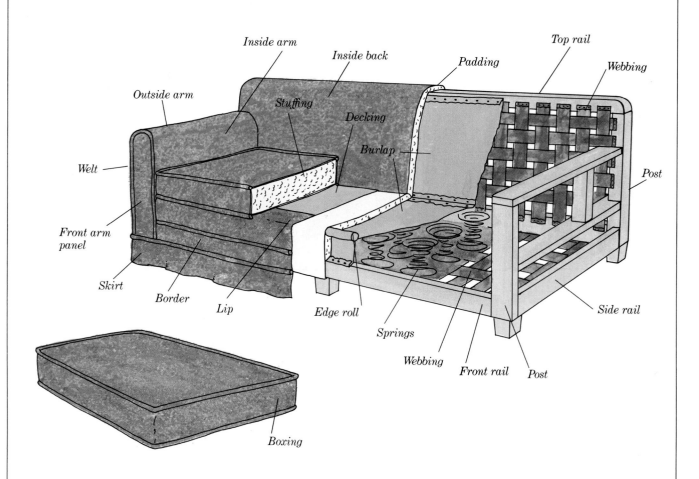

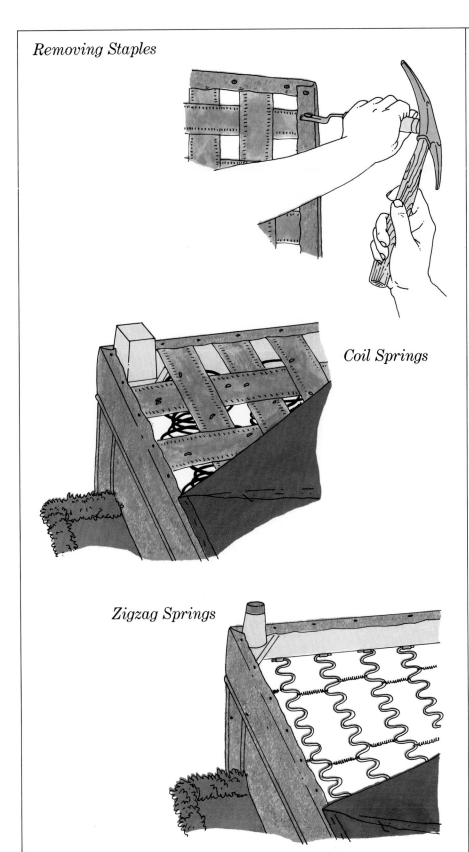

*Removing Staples*

*Coil Springs*

*Zigzag Springs*

T he first step in dismantling a piece of furniture in preparation for reupholstering is to remove the outer cover or covers. (You may find more than one.) This section describes the pieces that you will be taking off.

Most furniture does not have to be stripped to the bare frame before being reupholstered. You will have to decide how far it is necessary to go. Base your decision on what you find as you remove each layer. You may decide to remove only the old outer fabric, leaving the original stuffing and adding a new layer of cotton padding. Or you may feel that while you're at it you should replace and strengthen certain parts before recovering the piece. Read through this chapter for guidelines on what to look for.

## Sequence of Removal

The individual sections that make up the cover of a sofa are listed below. They appear in the order in which you should remove them. To avoid damaging the front edge of the frame when removing staples and tacks, do not press the tool against the edge of the rail. Instead, pry away from the frame, always working from the outside to the inside of the wooden rail. Also, when using a hammer in combination with a staple remover, use the center edge of the hammer to keep from hitting your knuckles.

### Dust Catcher

Turn your piece of furniture upside down on the upholsterer's horses (see Tools & Supplies, page 18) or on the table on which you plan to do the work. Remove the fabric covering the bottom. This serves as a dust catcher,

35

and it also finishes the bottom neatly. Sometimes cambric (a gauzy fabric, usually black in color) is used here. Later, when you are ready to replace this piece, any fabric can be used, even the old piece, if it is in good shape. Underneath the dust catcher you will find one of two types of springs: coil or zigzag. Depending on the piece of furniture, the springs will be either exposed or covered with webbing.

Once the springs and webbing are exposed, you can decide whether they need repair and, if so, how much. This knowledge will help you decide what tools to buy for the project. If you find that the inner structure of your piece is in good shape, you can probably get by with only a few tools.

### Skirt

Remove the skirt, if there is one, from around the bottom edge of the piece. Also remove any cording. This can be done with ordinary pliers.

### Outside Back

To remove the outside back, start at the bottom and work up the sides to the top.

An easy way to remove the back is simply to cut it loose around the outside edge using a knife. This means, however, that you will not be able to use the piece as an accurate pattern for the new cover. A better method is to pull the fabric off the frame using pliers or a staple remover for stubborn areas. Pull up and twist slightly as you go.

As you remove the fabric, be sure to remove all of the old staples, even the buried ones. This will provide a cleaner finish. Once the wood is exposed, examine it and flatten with a hammer any small pieces of staple that may be left. These can tear your fabric and scratch your fingers.

### Front Panels

If your piece has them, remove the front arm panels.

*Removing Outside Back*

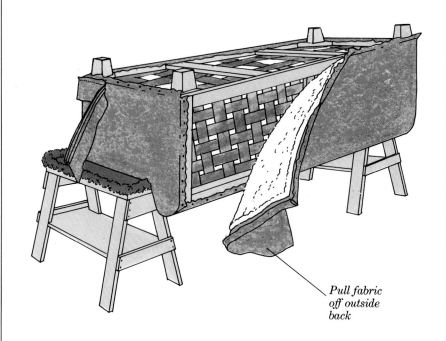

Pull fabric off outside back

*Removing Outside Arms*

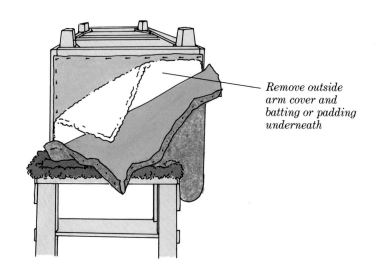

Remove outside arm cover and batting or padding underneath

### Outside Arms

Now remove the outside arm cover. Remove the batting or stuffing carefully. Check over the padding when you remove it and, if it is in good condition, save it. If you decide to reuse the old padding, it is best to place an additional layer over it to prevent any accumulated dirt from soiling your new fabric. Next remove the burlap or other filler material.

Make sure that all fabric and tacks are removed from the bottom rails.

### Lip and Border

The lip forms the front edge of the piece, and the border (if there is one) is a separate piece of fabric attached below the lip. If your project has both a border and a lip, first detach the border and then the lip from the bottom of the frame.

### Stretcher Material

Stretchers are pieces of inexpensive fabric sewn on to the cover fabric to add length for tacking. They are used to avoid wasting decorative fabric in areas that will not be visible.

To remove the stretchers, turn your project right side up making sure . If you are using upholsterer's horses, be sure that the legs of your project are securely positioned in the troughs. Remove the stretcher material from the inside rail.

### Removing Stretcher Material

*Pull stretcher material free from inside rail*

### Inside Back

Pull off the cover from the inside back, using pliers or a staple remove as necessary.

### Inside Arms

Remove the cover from the inside arms, and roll back the batting to see if any work needs to be done to theunderlying structure. It may be necessary to restretch the webbing or replace the burlap to restore the furniture to its original condition. The batting on the inside of the arms can either be removed or left rolled back out of the way while you are working in this area. If the batting is in poor condition, remove it completely and replace it with new batting later.

### Seat

Remove the seat and the lip, which are sewn together. As all pieces of fabric have been untacked at this point, you can remove an attached cushion, if there is one.

## Final Check

Once all of the old cover sections have been removed you can judge the condition of the stuffing. If it looks good, you may decide to stop dismantling at this point. This is fine as long as the frame feels sturdy and the springs and webbing appear to be sound. However, if you have any doubts about the general condition of your piece of furniture, now is the time to check it out thoroughly. It would be a total waste of time, effort, and fabric to recover a piece that will collapse before you have time to enjoy the fruits of your labor.

Be careful that you don't throw away any of the old fabric sections when clearing up. Iron and carefully label each piece for future reference.

# REPAIRING WEBBING

*O*nce *the piece of furniture is stripped of the fabric, roll back the padding and check the webbing. Webbing is often used under the springs of the seat; you may also find it in the back and sides of the piece.*

*If the webbing is still taut, you can leave it as is, but if it is sagging, you will have to restretch it or, as a last resort, replace it. For either task you will need webbing pliers or a webbing stretcher.*

In addition to supporting the springs in chairs and sofas, webbing is also sometimes used as the sole support in the seats and backs of wood-framed furniture. You can use the basic steps given here to strengthen or replace webbing in this type of furniture as well.

## Restretching Webbing

If the webbing is sagging but seems basically sound, it simply needs to be tightened. Starting in the center, remove the tacks from one end of a piece that runs from front to back. Stretch the webbing with a webbing stretcher or webbing pliers and re-tack the webbing, following the directions given below. Undo and restretch the strips one at a time, working from the center toward the sides, alternating between left and right of the center. Working this way keeps the pressure of the seat springs under control.

## Using Webbing Pliers

When using webbing pliers, grip the end of the webbing with the pliers and stretch it until taut, taking care not to bow the wood frame. Place four number 10 tacks across the webbing, as shown opposite, and hammer them in. Fold the end of the webbing back over the tacks and, for additional strength, secure it with four more tacks to hold down the folded piece of webbing. Stagger the second row of tacks so that you are not nailing on top of the first. Tighten each strip that runs front to back in this manner. Repeat the process with the webbing that runs from side to side across the piece of furniture.

## Using a Webbing Stretcher

If you are using a webbing stretcher and find that there is not enough webbing for a good grip, you can get the extra length needed by attaching an additional piece of webbing or a strip of strong fabric cut to the same width as the webbing. Thread a spear-point needle or an upholsterer's skewer through the two pieces to join them.

Brace the webbing stretcher against the rail with the pointed end facing you. With the points piercing the webbing, pull the pointed end of the stretcher toward you until the stretcher is horizontal and the webbing is taut. You may have to move the points to a different place in the webbing several times before achieving the correct tension. When you have finished, the webbed area should feel very hard and have very little give to it.

Tack the webbing down as described in Using Webbing Pliers. If you attached an extra piece to lengthen the webbing, place the first four tacks into the rail, remove the needle and extra piece of webbing, and then fold the webbing back and hammer in the remaining four tacks.

## Reinforcing Webbing

If the webbing is in poor condition, it should be reinforced.

The position of the original webbing was chosen strategically to support the springs, so to avoid disturbing them, it is best to place new webbing over the old. Begin tacking the strips that run from front to back, working from the center as described in Restretching Webbing. Place a new strip over an old one, stretching it as tight as possible with your pliers or stretcher, but taking care that the framework does not bow. Secure the new webbing with tacks, being careful to avoid the old ones. When adding the lengthwise strips, tack one end down and then weave the webbing in the same manner as the old webbing, or as shown in the illustration opposite.

## Replacing Webbing

If the old webbing is truly falling apart and you feel it should be removed, mark its position on the wood frame and remove and replace one strip at a time, cutting the twine attaching the springs to the old webbing as you go. This ensures that the webbing is positioned over the springs correctly and also keeps the spring pressure under control while you are working. You will resew the coil-spring bottoms to the webbing after all the new webbing is in place (see page 41).

## Restretching Webbing

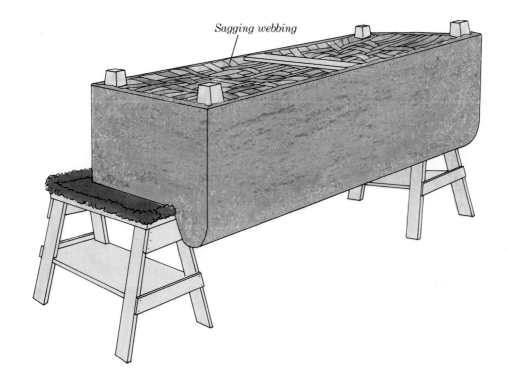

Sagging webbing

Restretch sagging webbing using webbing pliers. Secure webbing with 4 tacks

Fold webbing back and hammer in 4 more tacks

If existing webbing is not long enough to grip, pin on an extra length

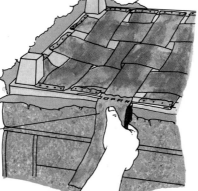

Brace stretcher against rail, points toward you. Tack webbing in place, then remove extra length

# SPRINGS

T he most important part of any chair or sofa is the seat, which is why it is important to take a good look at the springs and webbing before recovering.

The two most common types of springs are zigzag springs and coil springs. Coil springs are considered the better of the two.

On some furniture you may find rubber strapping springs. If these need repair, it is recommended that you have the job done professionally.

## Zigzag Springs

Zigzag springs are secured to the outer edges of the frame by metal clips. Two problems you may find are that the rail has split, or the clips have pulled out. In either case, have the repair done professionally because the clips that hold the springs may be hard to find. The springs themselves are very strong and seldom break, but if the clips have broken loose from the frame, no amount of retying through the center with twine will correct the situation. The springs must be tightly attached to the frame.

If the twine that runs from side to side is broken, you can repair it yourself using spring twine. Correct tying across the springs prevents them from tipping sideways.

You may find that rows of zigzag springs are connected with small coil springs. If one of these spring connections is broken, you can remove it and still retie the springs going from side to side with the twine.

To tie zigzag springs from side to side, start with a tie across the center and then work toward either end. Make sure that the ties are spaced no less than 4 inches apart on the seat.

Tie the springs from side to side. Attach the twine to the center of one side rail by making a knot and driving a size 16 tack through the center of it into the frame. Pass twine over then under the first spring and tie a knot. Repeat across all the springs. The twine between the springs should be taut, but not so tight that it distorts the springs. When you reach the opposite side of the frame, fasten the twine securely.

*Zigzag Springs Connected with Springs*

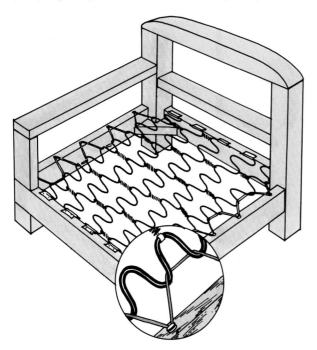

*Zigzag Springs Connected with Twine*

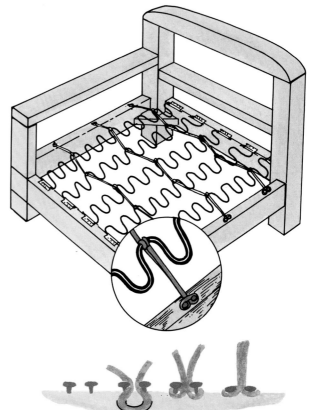

## Coil Springs

Coil springs are attached to a webbed bottom and tied together on top to hold them firmly in place. If the webbing is in need of repair, you must tighten or replace it. Then you can restitch the coils to the webbing. If twine securing the tops of the coils has rotted or worked loose, it is best to retie over the old twine. Even if only a few ties are broken, you will end up with a smoother surface by retying all the springs.

### Replacing a Spring

If one of the springs is broken, cut the twine around it, leaving the others intact. Remove the broken spring, and replace it with a new one of the same size. Springs vary in size, so take the old one along when purchasing a replacement.

### Repairing Webbing

Keeping all springs tied in place on the top of the seat, reweb the bottom as described on page 38. Then turn the piece over to reset the springs. They should be in an upright position, with the center of the coil straight up and down.

### Sewing Springs to Webbing

Check that the springs are set correctly in place. Attach or restitch them to the webbing.

Starting with a corner spring, tack the end of a long piece of twine to the frame. With a long needle, go up through the webbing, over the base of the spring, and back through the webbing. (If you use a double-pointed needle, you won't have to turn it over to go back through.)

Tie a knot to hold the stitch firmly in place. Reinsert the needle at a point about a third of the way around the inner edge of the coil, coming back through and knotting the twine as you did at the first point. Make your third stitch completing the triangle close to the edge of the next spring. After locking this stitch in place, move on to the next coil. Each spring should have three ties. Repeat for each coil, following the pattern shown in the illustration.

Once the springs are securely attached to the webbing, tie the end of the twine around a tack and hammer it into the frame.

### Retying Springs

Turn the piece of furniture over to work on the twine that secures the springs at the top of the seat. Check to be sure the springs are all in an upright position, evenly spaced.

To resecure the springs, first tie from back rail to front rail, starting with a center row of springs and working toward the sides (see illustrations on pages 42 and 43). Then tie from side to side, again starting in the center of the rail. For added strength you may finish with diagonal ties.

If there is a crown in the center of the seat, the springs on either side can be tied to create a smooth arc.

*Edgewire.* Before you start retying, look at the edgewire, if there is one.

This is a strip of metal that runs all around the outside and provides a framework for the springs. The edgewire should remain securely in place; do not remove it. If the clips holding edgewire are loose, pinch them together tightly with pliers.

*Knotting.* Make all knots in this manner: Go over the wire, around and under the wire, and through the loop forming the knot. Hold the loop with your thumb after the twine is drawn taut and pull with your other hand, securing the knot into position on the spring.

Going over and under the wire is important because it prevents the knot from slipping. When the knot is pulled tight, pull on it again to be sure it's really tight. Remember to keep all springs straight up and down while tying.

### Side-to-Side Rows

When all the front-to-back rows are completed, retie the rows of springs from side to side, again starting in the center of the rail. On these rows, cut your twine to a length twice the actual measurement of the frame.

Make a knot 9 inches from the end of the piece of twine and tack it to the center of one of the side rails. Then tie straight across the center row of springs in the same manner as described for tying the front-to-back rows. When tying off the excess pieces of twine, secure them on the top coil of the spring, as before.

## Retying Coil Springs

1. Cut a length of twine 3 times the actual length of frame and knot it 9 inches from one end. Place a tack in center of knot and, starting in center of back rail, hammer in tack leaving 9-inch tail hanging free

3. Proceed to front of same spring, but to the top coil, going over the wire then under the wire. Secure with another knot

5. On next-to-last spring, drop down one coil and tie on front edge

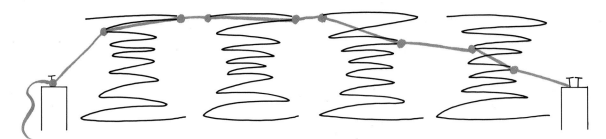

2. Loop around second coil down of first spring, even if the old tie is somewhere else. Make a knot

4. Loop twine around wire of next spring in line. Secure it at back of top coil with another knot. Then bring twine straight across coil to front and make a knot. Continue in this manner on top of springs until you reach the next-to-last spring from front

6. On final spring in the line, drop down to third coil at back of spring for first knot, and down to fourth coil on front edge for second knot. Hammer two tacks partway into front rail centering them on spring. Pull twine between tacks and, pushing down on center of spring with one hand, pull on twine to adjust

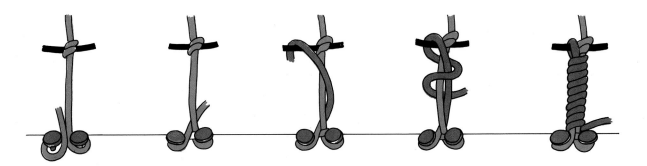

7. Secure twine around tacks, weaving it around them. End with twine pointing back toward spring. Tack down securely

*8. Slip twine over fourth coil on first spring. Keeping twine taut, wrap it around the double row of twine leading back toward the tacks. Push loops as close together as possible*

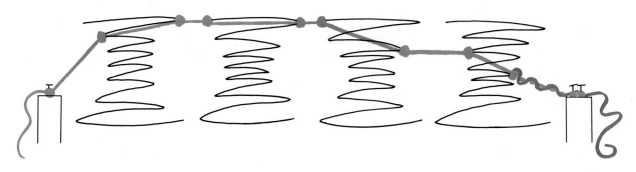

*9. Place a third tack in front of other two*

*11. Loop twine around front edge of top coil, adjusting for correct height and placement. Make knot and tighten*

*10. Loop twine, making a hitch, which will result in twine returning to front edge. Tighten*

*12. Loop twine around back edge of same spring without knotting, and move on to back edge of second spring. Make knot*

*14. Bring twine down to third coil in front spring. Knot at front edge and tighten. On front rail, add a tack next to the first three and wrap twine around tack so that it heads back toward spring*

*13. Still working on top, bring twine to front edge of same spring and set a knot, catching the first twine in it. Before tightening, pull on cord to bring front spring in line with front of frame. Then draw knot tight*

*15. Twist twine around and under tacked-down twine, then bring it up and tie securely to front edge of top coil of first spring. This adds strength along the front area*

## Side View of Steps 12–15

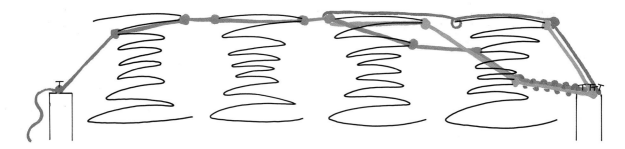

# STRENGTHENING LOOSE JOINTS

**O**ne of the most common faults of older furniture is loose joints. A good glue is often all that's required to solve the problem.

Avoid disassembling the piece unless joints need to be strengthened and repaired or unless you need to remove and replace a section. If a repair looks complicated, you may want to leave it to a professional.

## Gluing Loose Joints

Shaky joints can be reglued without taking the piece apart if the loose joints are not filled with dirt and old glue. The simplest way to do this is by applying glue with a toothpick and rocking the piece to work the glue into the joint. If possible, turn the piece so that the joint is vertical—that way, the glue penetrates to the bottom of the joint.

Glue may also be injected into a loose joint with a plastic squeeze bottle, a glue injector, or glue needle.

If the joint is not loose enough to accept an applicator, drill a small hole at an angle to and through the joint. The hole should be about $1/16$ inch and placed where it will not show. Inject glue into the drill hole. Continue to force glue in until it overflows. Wipe off excess, clamp the joint, and let the glue set.

### Types of Glue

Whatever glue you choose, first read the manufacturer's recommendations. Minor details about suitability and application can affect the bond.

*White glue.* This is the most popular and effective general adhesive.

*Yellow glue.* Yellow glue is an improved version of white glue. It bonds more strongly than white, fills gaps better, and dries more quickly.

*Epoxy.* This two-part waterproof glue is the strongest adhesive available. Epoxy can be used lavishly as a filler and sanded after it sets.

*Contact cement.* This adhesive is mostly used to attach veneers. Position pieces with care as contact cements set almost instantly.

*Animal and fish glues.* These glues are still used by purists who restore antiques. However, unless you insist on authenticity, there is no good reason to use these obsolete products.

*Miscellaneous glues.* Other glues used on furniture include resorcinol, urethane, and various plastic resin substances. However, none of these have significant advantages over the previously mentioned products.

## Disassembling Joints

It may be possible to simply pull the old loose joint apart. If it is not, use a rubber mallet or hammer to break apart the glue bonds and protect the surface that you strike. A block of softwood padded with a sheet of cork is best, but a block thickly wrapped with newspaper will do quite well.

Place the protective block as near as possible to the joint to be separated. If possible, hold the piece up slightly with one hand (about ½ inch from the surface it is resting on) while striking downward on the block with the other.

If the glue bond doesn't break easily, don't smash it with excessive force. Instead, use a lever to pry the joint open. To make a lever, you need two narrow pieces of wood. The combined length should be slightly longer than the distance between the parts to be separated.

Cut a concave *V* in the end of one piece and shape the end of the other into a convex *V*; the two pieces should fit together. Position the two pieces so that the unshaped ends are as near as possible to the joints to be separated. Use cork, softwood blocks, or folded newspaper to pad the ends of the lever that touch the furniture. Fit the V-shaped ends of the lever together to form a joint. Press downward on the V-joint with your hands, gradually straightening the lever and forcing the glued joints to separate.

### Disassembling Pinned Joints

Some glued joints are pinned, and the first job is to find the pin and remove it. If you can't see the head, look for a plug or filled hole where the pin has been countersunk. Tap the pin through with a nail set or pull it out with a pair of nippers.

If the joint has been pinned with a wooden dowel and plugged, the plug should be pried out with an ice pick or an awl, or drilled out with an electric drill set to reverse. If possible, tap out the pinning dowel by lightly hammering on a dowel of slightly smaller diameter or drill out the old dowel. Use a doweling jig to keep the new hole straight.

### Disassembling Dovetail Joints

Take special care when breaking the glue bond in a dovetail joint—the interlocking fingers of the joint will break if the force is applied at an angle. Force the joint open by striking one element of the joint so that the fingers are driven straight out.

## Repairing Joints

Sometimes glue alone is not enough. This is the case when a tenon has broken or dried out and shrunk.

A loose or broken tenon can be shimmed with small pieces of veneer. Thin strips of birch, which can be found in stores specializing in model-making supplies, make excellent shims. Cut out and glue a shim to the tenon. When glue is dry, test for fit. If it is still loose, glue on another shim; if it is too tight, sand as necessary.

Another way to correct a loose-fitting tenon is to wrap it with cord or any other material that will soak up glue. Or, if you don't want to disassemble the joint, you can saw a deep slot and hammer in a wedge.

# REFORMING THE INTERIOR

Now you can start to rejuvenate what is at present a rather sad-looking piece of furniture. First you cover the inner seat, inside back, and, possibly, the inside arms with burlap.

## Burlap

Burlap is a loosely woven material made of jute that can be found in most fabric stores that carry upholstery materials. For this purpose, select a heavy burlap.

### Cutting and Measuring

When cutting burlap, it is a good idea to make a small snip and pull out a lengthwise or crosswise thread. The resulting gap will give you a perfectly straight cutting line that you can just follow with your scissors.

To determine the dimensions of the burlap seat, measure across the largest portion of the front of the frame, from outside arm to outside arm. Allow 4 inches extra (2 inches at each end) on this and all other pieces; this excess will be turned over when tacked into place. To measure the depth of the seat, start at the front rail and go up and over springs and across seat to the back rail; add 4 inches to this measurement. Cut a piece of burlap to these measurements, leaving one selvage intact.

If the inside back needs recovering, measure it from top to bottom and from side to side, remembering to add 2 inches all around (that is, add 4 inches to each dimension).

If you are replacing the burlap on the inside arms, measure framework in the same way, or take measurements from one of the original pieces of burlap. The latter method is preferable if the arm is shaped.

### Tacking the Inner Seat

Place selvage on top of front rail, turning under ½ inch. Using the selvage on the front gives you a straight line to follow and makes the front neat. Starting in the center and working toward sides, tack down front edge. Place tacks approximately 2 inches apart, and hammer them into the center of the rail to avoid splitting wood. Continue until front rail is completed.

Stretch burlap smoothly across springs to back rail, turn over excess, and tack burlap to center of back rail, again placing tacks 2 inches apart.

To cut around posts or rails, fold burlap back and mark shape of the obstruction with chalk before cutting. To prevent burlap from tearing, make V-shaped cuts.

Make a neat pleat at front corners and cut away excess material. Tack edges to side rails, and the inner seat cover is complete.

*Estimating Amount of Burlap Needed*

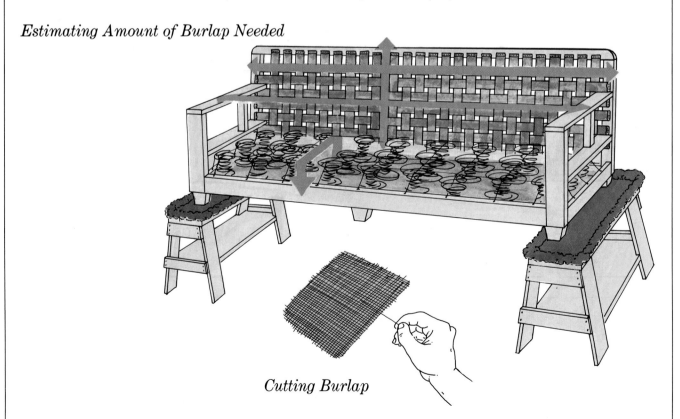

*Cutting Burlap*

*Attaching Burlap to Inner Seat*

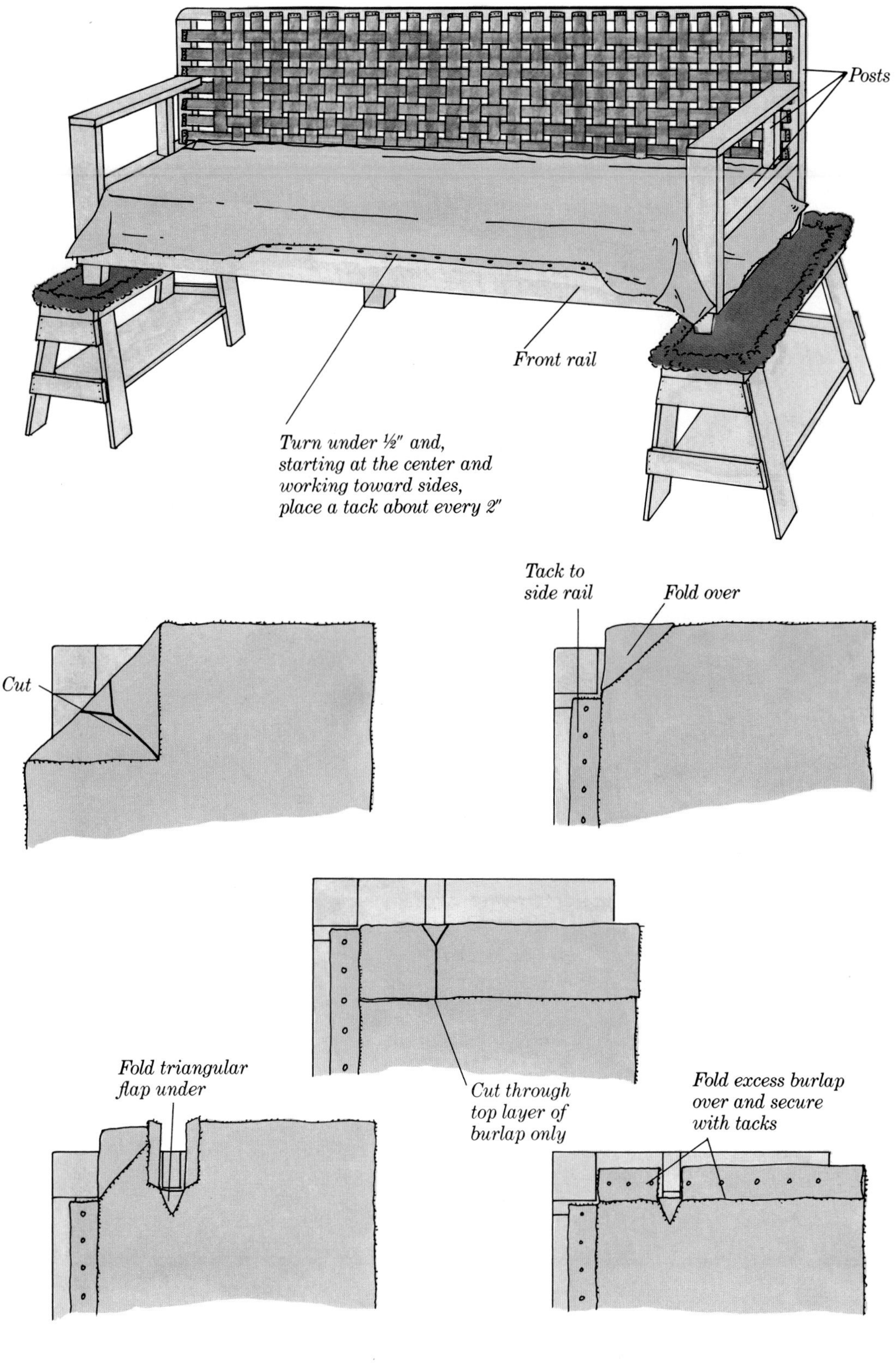

*Posts*

*Front rail*

*Turn under ½" and, starting at the center and working toward sides, place a tack about every 2"*

*Cut*

*Tack to side rail*

*Fold over*

*Fold triangular flap under*

*Cut through top layer of burlap only*

*Fold excess burlap over and secure with tacks*

### Tacking the Inside Back and Arms

Attach the inside back from bottom rail to top rail, then side rail to side rail, turning over the excess and tacking it as you did for the seat cover. If you are replacing the cover on the inside arms, repeat this procedure working from bottom side rail to top side rail and then front to back.

Now that the burlap is securely tacked to the wooden framework, you are ready to stitch it in place, using twine and a curved needle.

### Stitching Burlap in Place

Sew around the outer edges, inserting the needle into the burlap and under the edgewire, then securing the stitch with a knot, as shown in the illustration. (If the piece of furniture is constructed without an edgewire, attach the cover to the springs.) These knotted stitches tie the burlap and edgewire tightly together.

### Attaching Burlap

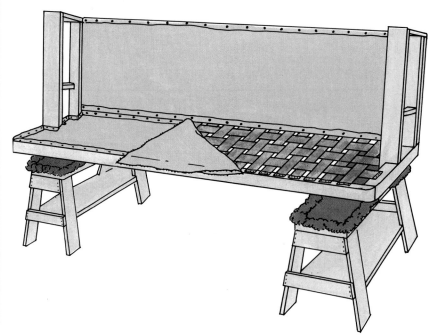

### Stitching Burlap

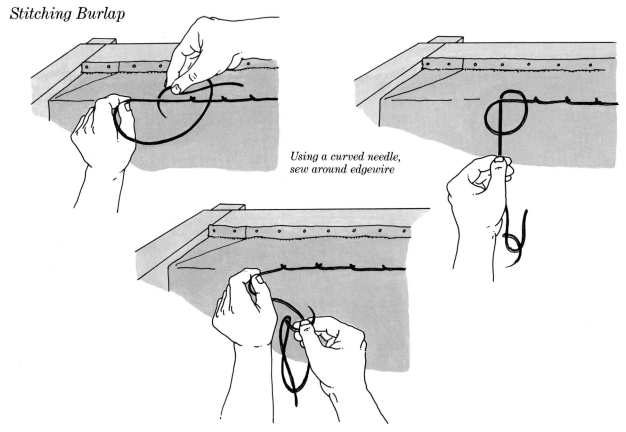

*Using a curved needle, sew around edgewire*

## Making Boxed Corners

Mark or crease burlap

Cut along mark or crease

Mark position of lip

Join the front and side edges into a fitted, boxed corner and sew them to each other and to the edgewire, using the same stitching method. Make a chalk line on the burlap 4½ inches in from the front wire or seat edge. This will give you a guideline when you are positioning the lip.

## Edge Roll

After the burlap cover is on, attach an edge roll, sometimes called fox edging, to the front edge of the seat. Edge roll looks like oversized welt cord; it is about 1½ inches in diameter with a ½-inch flat backing, or flange. It has a burlap cover and can be filled with various materials including paper, hair, cotton, or jute; all work well, but jute is recommended.

Placing an edge roll along the front edge of your sofa or chair serves several purposes. It softens the hard edge, it protects your upholstery fabric from rubbing against the front wire, and it builds up a lip that prevents the seat cushions from sliding forward. Remember—the front of your piece of furniture will get the most wear.

In many cases, you will find that you can reuse the original edge roll, but if it is in poor condition and you

wish to replace it, you can purchase new edge roll at an upholstery supply store. Measure your old piece for size and length.

The following directions describe how to attach edge roll to a sofa or chair with a straight edge. On a curved piece of furniture, edge roll can either be sewn in the same manner or tacked in place depending on how it was originally attached. To round the corners, cut small V-shaped notches in the back flange. Space cuts close together for a tight arc and slightly wider apart for a shallower one.

Place the edge roll along the front edge so that it overhangs the edgewire by approximately ¼ inch. Using a curved needle, insert the needle into the back of the edge roll as close to the actual roll as possible, with the ½-inch backing resting flat on the burlap seat cover. Bring the needle under the edgewire and through the front, so that the thread encircles the roll. Secure with a slipknot in the front, as shown. Space the stitches approximately 1½ inches apart. Continue along the entire front edge until the roll is completely attached.

Still using the curved needle and twine, sew the flat backing of the roll to the burlap. This will prevent the backing from flopping forward.

### Attaching Edge Roll

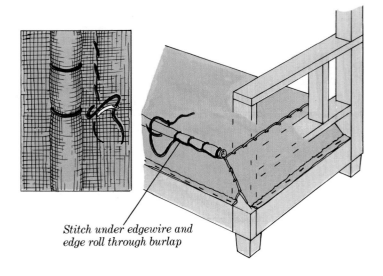

Stitch under edgewire and edge roll through burlap

# ATTACH-ING THE NEW COVER

T*he following directions for covering a piece of furniture with new fabric apply to most chairs and sofas. Within the basic directions, you will find variations that take into account furniture of different shapes and whether or not the piece will have a skirt.*

*Included are techniques for achieving a snug fit, for shaping fabric around posts and rails, and for tacking fabric permanently in place after it's properly positioned. The pieces of the old cover that you carefully removed and labeled will be a great help as you attach the new one. Be sure to add new sections in the sequence indicated.*

*Many people who have never tackled an upholstery project think that it will involve a lot of sewing. They do not realize that most of the fabric sections are tacked or stapled in place. However, when a section does need to be sewn, a circular needle is an essential piece of equipment.*

# RECOVERING THE SEAT

The first part of your sofa or chair to be recovered is the seat. You will need to machine-stitch a section of fabric to fit around boxed corners of the lip. Also, the lip edge should be padded to raise it slightly higher than the decking and to create a smooth angle over the edge roll.

An optional touch, if you are using plain decking fabric, is to conceal it by placing strips of the decorative outer fabric over the decking where the cushions meet.

## Sequence of Work
Recover the seat using the techniques that follow in the order in which they are presented.

### Shaping the Corner
To shape the boxed corner of the lip, cut a piece to match the example shown, substituting your own measurements and remembering to add seam allowances.

Fold the lip right sides together so that the cut edges are even. Seam these edges together, backstitching to reinforce the front corners. Cut away the excess fabric close to the stitches and press the seam open to eliminate bulk.

### Covering the Decking
Although it is not absolutely necessary, you can attach fabric to conceal the decking.

If you are covering a sofa and you are using a plain fabric for the decking, you will probably want to add strips of your outer cover fabric at the points where the seat cushions meet. These fabric strips will conceal the decking if the cushions separate.

## Shaping the Corner

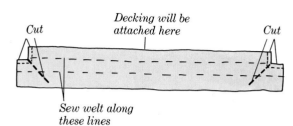

Cut

Decking will be attached here

Cut

Sew welt along these lines

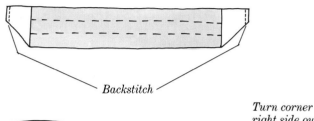

Backstitch

Turn corner right side out

## Adding Matching Strip

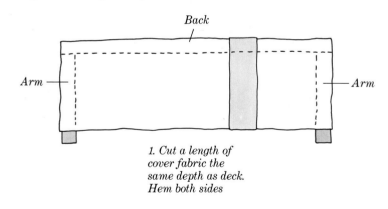

Back

Arm

Arm

*1. Cut a length of cover fabric the same depth as deck. Hem both sides*

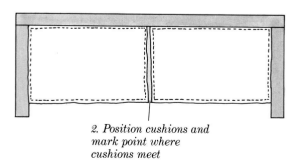

*2. Position cushions and mark point where cushions meet*

*3. Lay fabric strip(s) in position. Place decking on top*

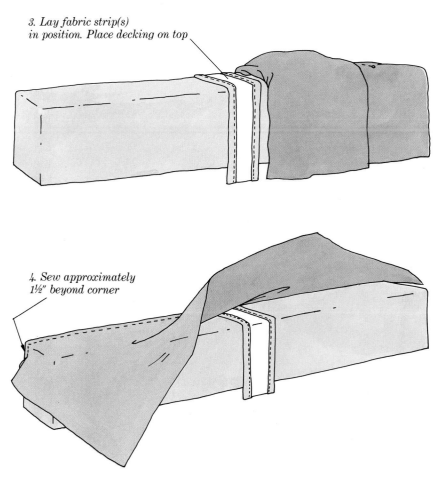

*4. Sew approximately 1½" beyond corner*

## Attaching Lip Padding

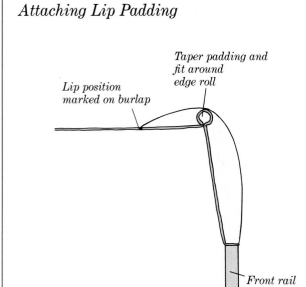

*Lip position marked on burlap*

*Taper padding and fit around edge roll*

*Front rail*

If used, the strips of the outer cover fabric should be attached to the decking at this point.

Cut the pieces 5 inches wide and long enough to reach from the lip to the back of the decking. Turn under and sew a ½-inch seam allowance on each side. To locate the correct placement of these strips, place your decking in position, set the cushions on top, and mark the decking at the points where the cushions meet. Center the strips over these marks. The strips will be sewn into the lip and decking seam and will be tacked to the back rail along with the decking.

### Sewing Decking to Lip

With right sides together, sew the decking to the lip section along the seat edge of the lip. Extend the stitches approximately 1½ inches past the corners of the lip.

### Padding the Lip

Place padding along the lip line marked on the burlap to the edge of the edge roll. Fill in or build up this padding to the height of the edge roll to form a gradual slope into the seat. Place another layer of padding over the first layer from the lip line, extending over the seat front.

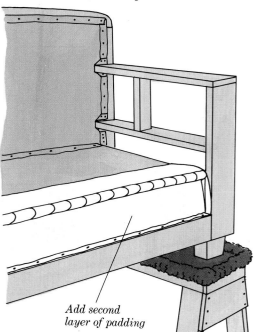

*Add second layer of padding*

## Attaching Lip and Decking

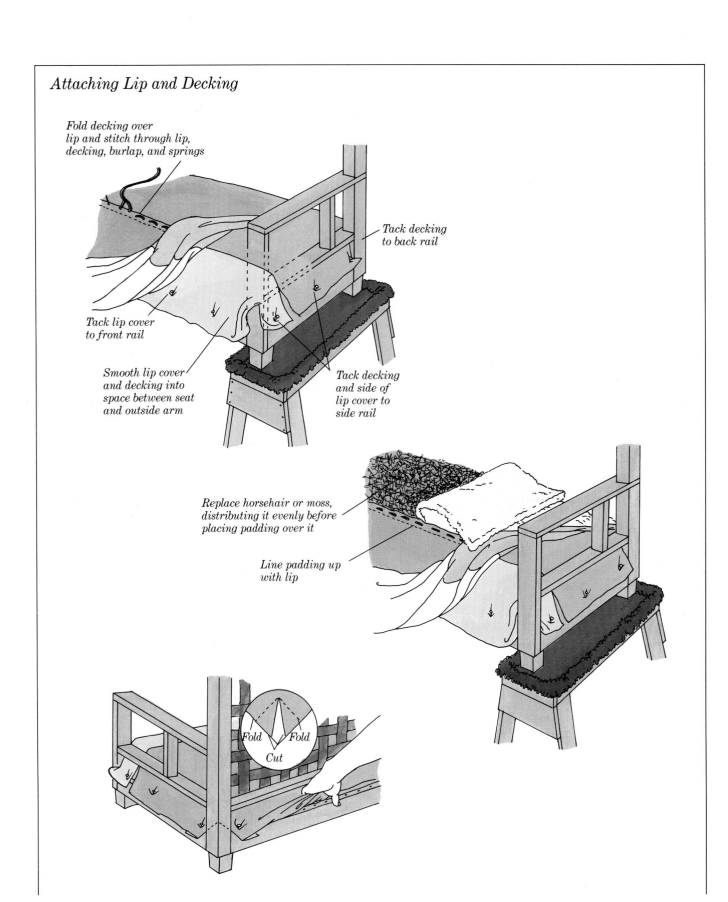

Fold decking over lip and stitch through lip, decking, burlap, and springs

Tack decking to back rail

Tack lip cover to front rail

Smooth lip cover and decking into space between seat and outside arm

Tack decking and side of lip cover to side rail

Replace horsehair or moss, distributing it evenly before placing padding over it

Line padding up with lip

Fold    Fold

Cut

### Attaching Lip and Decking

After the padding is in place, fit the lip and decking onto the piece of furniture. Line up the stitched seam of the lip and decking with the chalk mark you made on the burlap; this is also where the padding now ends.

Smooth the fabric by pulling the excess into the space between the seat and inside arm. Place a temporary tack under the rail to hold the fabric in place.

With the decking fabric folded back over the lip, make sure that the seam is even with the line on the burlap and, using twine and a curved needle, sew in the seam allowance, parallel to the seam, stitching through the lip and decking seam allowance, the burlap, and the springs.

### Padding the Seat

If you removed horsehair or moss from the seat of your sofa or chair, replace it at this point. Be sure that it is distributed evenly before you place the new padding over it.

Line the padding up with the lip, and tuck the excess into the framework at the sides and back. Make sure that the padding is evenly tucked against the sewn edge at the lip. Place the decking back over the padded seat.

### Stretching the Decking

Smooth the decking over the seat area, fitting it tightly into position.

Pull the excess fabric to the back and sides, keeping the fabric on the seat tight.

### Cutting Around Obstructions

Cut the fabric to fit around any obstructing wooden rails. To make these cuts, fit the fabric closely around the post, fold back the fabric, and mark the shape of the obstruction on the fabric with chalk.

After marking the cuts, make a slit to the corner edge of the wood rail. Make V-shaped cuts just inside of your chalk lines, so that the fabric fits around the corner edge of the wood rail, as shown in the illustration. Be careful not to cut too deeply; it is better to make a cut that is too small and then snip it deeper, if necessary. Fold the excess fabric under; do not cut it off.

### Tacking the Decking

Use number 3 tacks to attach the fabric to the rails unless you are working on a delicate frame, in which case use number 2 tacks. The back of the decking is the first to be tacked down. Starting in the center and working toward the sides, tack the decking to the top of the back rail (to which the burlap is already secured). As you tack, pull the fabric gently to keep the decking stretched tightly over the seat. Pull the fabric toward the sides slightly as well. When the back is completely tacked down, trim off the excess fabric.

### Tacking the Lip

Move to the front of the furniture to tack down the lip. Starting in the center and working toward the sides, tack the fabric along the middle of the underside of the bottom rail if there is no border. Keep the lip fabric smooth and tight as you work.

Tack the excess fabric at the lower front corners to the front rail. Molding the shape of your corners, pull the fabric tightly through the sides of the furniture. Trim and fold the fabric around the legs as described under Cutting Around Obstructions.

Tack the sides of the lip and decking to the bottom of the side rails, making sure the boxed corners remain smooth in the front and pulling the fabric around the arm rails. Fold the excess fabric around the rails and tack it to the bottom rail. When the back, front, and sides are completely secured, you are ready to attach the border, if any.

### Cutting Around Obstructions

*Fold back fabric and mark shape of obstruction with chalk*

*Cut and fold to fit around post*

*Tack sides of lip and decking to side rails*

## Borders

Some pieces of furniture have a border extending across the front from the lip edge to the bottom framework. There may also be a lip and border in addition to the skirt.

If you are not applying a skirt, proceed as follows: Make welt following the instructions on page 28. Sew the welt to the top of the border. Trim away any excess fabric that extends more than ½ inch beyond the tacks that secure the lip. To be sure that the border will be straight, make a chalk mark ½ inch up from the bottom edge of the lip. Line up the border fabric and welt with the chalk line, place a strip of cardboard along the seam edge, and pin-tack in place. (To pin-tack, drive the tack only partway in.) Make sure that the border pattern matches the lip. When you are satisfied with the positioning, tack the border permanently into place.

Cover the area from the cardboard strip to the bottom rail with two layers of padding, smoothing it out evenly. Tack the border to the underside of the bottom front rail, clipping and folding the fabric to fit around the legs. Tack the sides of the border to the center of the front rails.

If you will be adding a skirt, use the old cover for measurements and as a guide to placement. Sew the welt to the fabric, tack the border into place, and add the padding, as previously described. Tack the border to the front rail and trim away the excess. The tacks will be covered by the skirt that will be attached later.

### Covering the Border

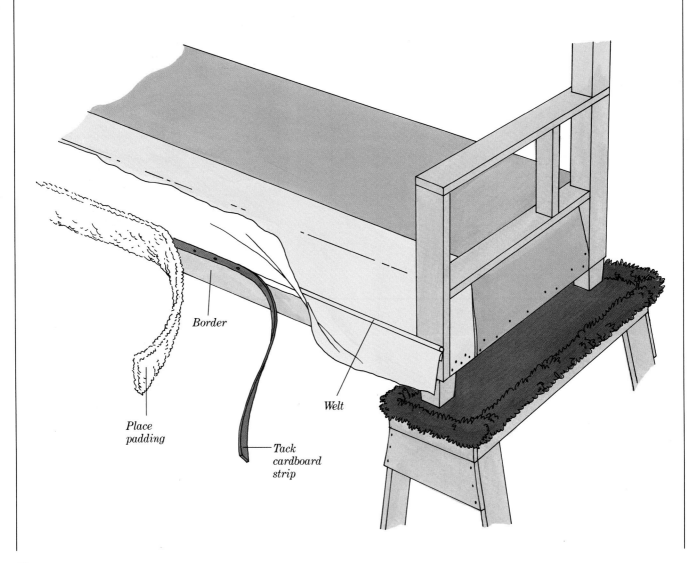

Border

Place padding

Welt

Tack cardboard strip

This section gives directons for covering two kinds of arms: scroll (rounded) and boxed. Scroll arms are the more difficult of the two, requiring careful arrangement of the padding to assure smooth lines, as well as precise tucking and cutting to fit the fabric. Some of the same techniques are used for covering boxed arms, but welting and possibly fitted panels are added.

The sequence for this stage of re-upholstering is the following: First cover the inside arms and inside back, then the outside arms and outside back.

## Scroll Arms

Following are directions for attaching the inside arm on a scroll or rounded arm. If your piece has boxed arms, turn to page 59.

If you are reusing the old padding, put it back into place on the arm and cover it with a layer of new padding. If it cannot be reused, replace it with enough layers of new padding to give the correct thickness. Press the padding between the rail and seat, and place it over the arm. Position the inside arm cover and pin-tack it lightly in place.

Tack the arm cover under the bottom of the arm rail, tacking the fabric to where the burlap and seat cover are tacked. Make sure the fabric lies flat and that the grain and the design are straight on the top of the arm.

Covering Inside of Scroll Arm

1. Tuck padding into space between rail and seat

2. Pull inside arm covering between seat and rail. Tack to bottom rail

## Attaching Scroll Arm Cover

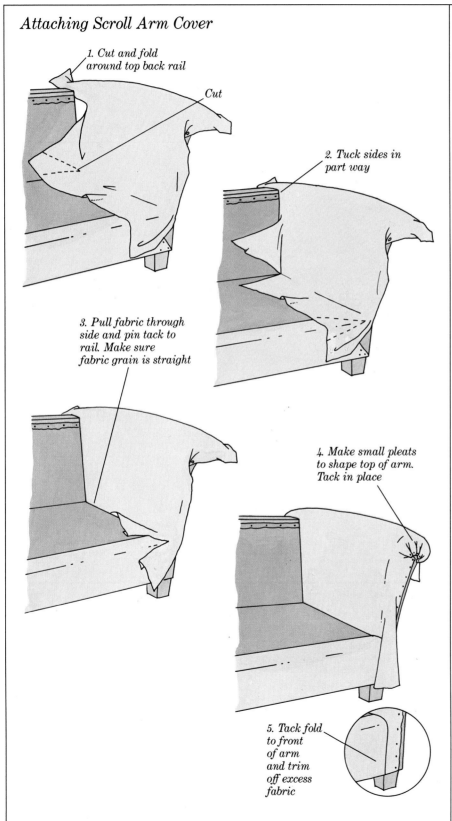

1. Cut and fold around top back rail

Cut

2. Tuck sides in part way

3. Pull fabric through side and pin tack to rail. Make sure fabric grain is straight

4. Make small pleats to shape top of arm. Tack in place

5. Tack fold to front of arm and trim off excess fabric

## Fitting Fabric Around Frame

Make the cuts to fit the fabric around the frame. Tuck the sides in partway, and make cuts as described in Cutting Around Obstructions, page 55; the cuts should be level with the inside rail edge. You may have to make adjustments later.

Pull the fabric through the sides and pin-tack it lightly to keep it in place. Check constantly to make sure that the grain is straight on the top of the arm. Make two cuts in the back, one at the top and one at the bottom, to fit the fabric around the back rail. Make a cut at the bottom of the top rail and then pin-tack lightly. At the bottom rail, make a V-shaped cut. Pull the fabric through at the bottom and then the sides of the back.

After checking that the design or grain is running evenly in both directions, tack the arm cover down permanently, starting with the front rail. Keep the excess batting smooth and even to the edge of the wood, avoiding lumps.

## Shaping Top of the Arm

To mold the fabric to fit the rounded shape of the top of the arm, make small pleats, working from the inside to the outside. All the pleats should radiate evenly. When all of the pleats are in place, tack the fabric down.

Another way of forming pleats is to baste along the edge to be pleated with twine and a needle, making ½-inch stitches around the circular shape. Gather the fabric, arranging the pleats as you gather. Pull on the twine to secure the pleats while you tack them into place.

Once the fabric is securely tacked to the front rail, trim off all excess fabric as close to the tacks as possible.

### Attaching Arm to Back Rail

When the front of the arm has been secured, tack the back section to the back rail. Carefully cut around any obstructions, measuring and marking as described earlier.

On many pieces of furniture, you will find an arm rail at the top of the outside arm of the sofa. This is usually 1½ to 2 inches wide. If your piece has this type of rail, simply tack your fabric to the side of the rail rather than underneath the rail. Later, the outside arm cover will be tacked over the inside arm cover either on this rail or under the rail, depending on the piece of furniture.

It is easier to tack the fabric under the arm if you turn the piece of furniture on its side.

### Pulling Inside Arm Through to Back

## Boxed Arms

Sew the welt to the front and top boxing of the arm (do this on the inside arm edge only); clip the corners to ease the welt. Sew the top and front boxing to the inside arm. With the padding in place on the top and front of the arm, fit the boxed cover over the arm. Pin-tack to check the placement, keeping the welt straight and even along the edge of the arm top and front. Tack the boxing fabric to the outer side of the arm and front rails, making a small pleat at the front corners. Tack under the bottom front rail. Pull the inside arm cover through the seat and back and attach it following the directions given on page 58. You will apply the outside arm cover later to complete the welt and boxed shape.

### Fitted Panels

Measure welt to go around the front panel. Sew the welt to the front panel, beginning at the bottom of the inside and continuing over the arm but stopping approximately 1 inch past the end of the outside curve. Sew the fabric for the inside arm to the panel and the welt, ending at the point at which you stopped attaching the welt. The top of the inside arm will be tacked to the top arm rail.

Place the padding on the inside arm and front of the piece of furniture. Fit the arm and front-panel section onto the furniture, pull the fabric to the back, and pin-tack it in place. Center the arm and front panel fabric on the top rail and then push the fabric through the seat and bottom rail. Proceed as for the scroll arm, tacking the fabric to the top outside rail and making cuts to fit the fabric around the rails before permanently tacking the bottom and sides down. Tack the front panel and the welt that is hanging free to the outside of the front rail, keeping the cord even down the front edge. You will attach the outside piece later.

*Cut to fit around rail*

*Cut to fit around rail*

### Attaching Front Arm to Rail

*Tack to underside of arm or to front of arm rail*

## Inside Back

Once the inside arm is in place, the inside back is next. Tack the inside back padding onto the top of the rail to hold it in place. Cover the tack heads with small pieces of padding to get rid of any indentations. To keep the line of the back smooth, do not extend the padding over the rail. Center the fabric with stretcher fabric attached (if desired), and pin-tack the section lightly in place, keeping the tacks toward the bottom at the back of the top rail. (You will also be tacking the outside back cover to this rail.) Pull the fabric through to the bottom rail, pin-tacking it lightly in place. After checking the placement, pull the fabric over the top of the back, starting in the center and easing it toward the sides. Tack it down as you go, stopping a short distance from the ends to cut around the rails. Keep the padding smooth at all times.

When the top is tacked down, pull the fabric at the bottom until the inside back fabric is taut and smooth. Now tack down the bottom. Place the tacks in the top part of the bottom rail, starting in the center and working toward the sides. Stop before reaching the ends so that you can cut around the rails. Make cuts at the top and bottom of the inside back as before by folding back the fabric and marking the shape with chalk. Make the V-shaped cut and check for fit.

Pull the remaining fabric through, fold it under, and tack it down.

### Inside Back with Boxing

If the back of the piece you are covering has a boxed shape, you must take a slightly different approach. Sew welt to the top and sides of the inside back and attach the boxing to this piece. Fit the section over the inside back and tack it onto the back rails in the same manner as for the rounded back. This is the method used for an inside arm that is boxed. You will attach the outside back and additional welt later.

## Padding and Covering the Inside Back

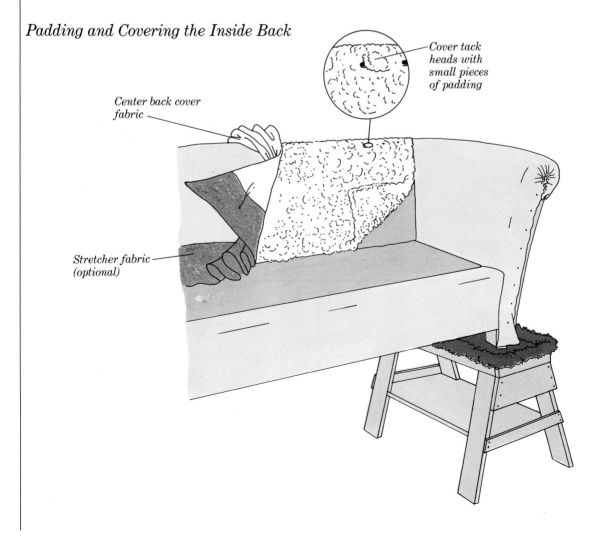

Center back cover fabric

Cover tack heads with small pieces of padding

Stretcher fabric (optional)

## Outside Arms

The following are directions for a piece that has separate front panels on the arm.

### Scroll Arms

When attaching outside arm sections, tack them either directly to the top rail or to the 1½- to 2-inch arm rail mentioned earlier, depending on your frame. Blind-tack outside arm to rail as follows: Holding top edge of the outer arm section in position against the furniture, flip lower part of fabric over the arm, so that you can tack the top into place. (The fabric is now upside down, right side against the furniture.) Place ½-inch cardboard tacking strip even with top edge of fabric, and tack both fabric and cardboard to top rail. Be sure to keep the pattern or grain straight at all times. The cardboard strip will ensure a straight edge.

As you near the sides, be sure to follow the line of the inside arm; it may alter at the ends. Fold under fabric before tacking ends in place.

The next step is to add a layer of burlap, tacking it over the top of the cardboard strip and to the outside and bottom rails. Cover burlap with a layer of padding; then tack outer cover fabric to underside of bottom rail, cutting diagonally for the corners of the legs. Bring fabric around and tack it to center of front arm rail. Then, tack it to the back rail, keeping the grain and design straight. Fold in corners of the arm, front and back, and around legs. Tack down. No raw edges should be visible.

### Boxed Arms

Although welt is measured and cut to fit around the front side and across the top, it is only sewn to the top of the outside arm section. Clip corners of welt for easing; this makes it easier to work with burlap and padding.

Once the welt is sewn to the top, position fabric so that cord runs along top of the arm. Tack top of outside arm down using cardboard tacking strip. Tack the free welt down on the outside of arm rails. Hand-sew sides together, using twine and a curved needle. Tack bottom of fabric under bottom rail and then to the back.

Tack on burlap and cover with padding. Draw cover fabric over and pin-tack to bottom of frame.

Fold in excess fabric and blind-sew sides of front using twine and a curved needle. Tack bottom of fabric under bottom rail and then to the back. Make an angled bias cut around back legs. Turn under excess.

### Fitted Panels

On a piece with fitted front arm panels, the outside arm section is treated in the same manner as for boxed arms but without the welt.

Using cardboard strip, blind-tack top to the same top rail to which inside arm was secured. Hand-sew sides; tack the bottom underneath.

## Outside Back

This section gives two methods for attaching the outside back cover. The first one uses fewer tacks when attaching fabric to rail, which helps avoid splitting wood.

### Method 1

Measure welt to fit around top and sides of back. Sew cord to top of outside back, stopping 1½ inches from the ends. (Let sides hang free.)

## Padding and Covering the Outside Arm

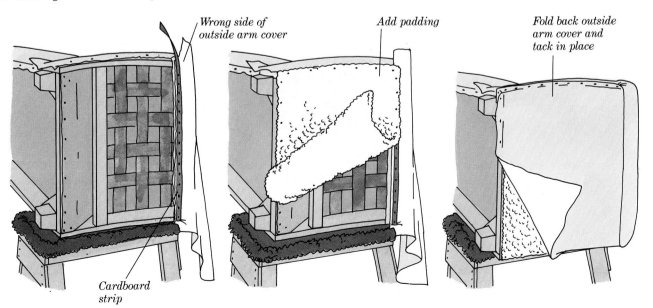

Wrong side of outside arm cover

Add padding

Fold back outside arm cover and tack in place

Cardboard strip

Place fabric and welt in position over the inside back seam allowance and tack. The seam should be level with top of the top back rail and the welt should be just above it. Flip lower part of fabric over the back of the furniture so that you can blind-tack fabric in place. Position cardboard tacking strip over both fabric and welt and, starting in the center, tack it in place. Stop 2 inches from ends and adjust welt to fit around corners. Clip so that it curves smoothly. Tack welt (the welt only) around corners and down the sides.

Add burlap and padding as described in Outside Arms. Fold under seam allowance; pin and blind-stitch fabric to welt.

## Method 2

Tack welt directly to frame along top and sides, lining it up with the edge of the rail. Once welt is in place, tack the fabric along the top edge, using a cardboard tacking strip. Fold seam allowance under. Pin and blind-stitch using twine and a curved needle.

When top and sides are attached, tack the bottom of the outside back to the underside of bottom rail.

# Front Arm Panels

Some pieces of furniture have a removable panel on the front of the arm, usually backed with plywood or cardboard. To recover front arm panels, remove all of the old fabric, stuffing, and tacks from the backing.

Before attaching the new cover, decide how you plan to reattach the panel to the piece of furniture. Read Attaching the Front Panels, below.

Cover backing with a light layer of padding on the front face only. Cut padding to shape so that it does not extend beyond the edges. Position fabric, making sure that the design is straight and centered and that the grain is straight. Fold edges of fabric around to the back.

Tack fabric in place with number 2 tacks, working on the sides first. If necessary, make small pleats around the curved top as you did for the

front arm. Cut away excess fabric.

To apply welt, measure all the way around the panel except along the bottom edge, add 1 inch, and cut a piece of welt to this length.

Tack welt to back of panel, starting at the bottom and leaving ½ inch extra to be secured underneath. Tack all around panel, except for bottom edge. Clip welt fabric to ease it around the curves. At bottom edges, push welt fabric up to expose some of the cord, cut exposed cord to the exact length of panel, and then fold and tack the ½ inch of excess welt fabric to back of panel.

## Attaching the Front Panels

There are two ways to attach the front panels. The first is with very fine finishing nails, which will pierce directly through the fabric. This method works well on coarsely woven fabrics. If the fabric is a thin or lightweight, use the second method.

*Method 1.* Plan on one nail close to the top and another close to the bottom and space the rest approximately 4 inches apart. Very carefully place the nails between threads in the front of the arm panel, piercing the fabric but taking care not to break

any threads. Holding the panel in position, drive nails through panel and into front arm. When the panel is secure, use a needle to move the threads back together until the hole can no longer be seen.

*Method 2.* Using nails that are about 1¼ inches long with a flat head (such as shingle nails), drive the nails just far enough into the panel to pierce through the plywood or cardboard. Place nailed panel in position on the arm and then hammer nails in just far enough to establish guide holes. Remove panel and cover it with stuffing, fabric, and welt, as described previously. Work carefully around nails. Place panel in position and hammer it into place.

If you are not adding a skirt, attach the dust cover now.

## Attaching the Back Panel

Flip lower part of panel over the front so that you can blind-tack the top of the back panel. Flip panel back over, and smooth into place.

At each side, fold under seam allowance and pin in place. Stretch panel and tack to underside of frame.

Using twine and a curved needle, blind-stitch down each side.

*Method 1*

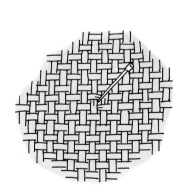

*Avoid breaking fibers.*
*Place finishing nails*
*between fibers*

*Method 2*

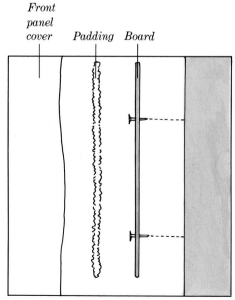

Front
panel
cover    Padding   Board

# ATTACHING SKIRT & DUST CATCHER

The method of attaching the skirt to the piece of furniture depends on the style of skirt you have made. See the Measuring and Sewing sections for information on making the skirt.

The final step before you turn to the cushions is attaching the dust catcher, a lightweight fabric tacked to the underside of the piece.

## Skirt

There are two methods for attaching a skirt, one for a skirt made in sections, the other for a one-piece skirt. Both methods require ½-inch cardboard tacking strip, tacks, and a hammer. If you would rather sew the skirt on by hand, position it in the same way as for tacking, but sew it in place with twine and a curved needle, making small blind stitches behind the welt. Turn your furniture as you work so that the skirt lies flat while you work under it.

### Method 1

These instructions are for a skirt that is made in separate sections.

With the welt in the center back, first fit the skirt, testing for size and correct placement of all pleats. When you are satisfied, cut off the excess cord so that the ends of the cord meet, and sew up the gap in the welt fabric through which the ends were left hanging.

Position the skirt on the furniture, placing all the pleats in their exact positions and matching the pattern, if necessary. Pin-tack the skirt into place at the corners and elsewhere as necessary to hold it in position while you work.

Begin tacking the skirt into place, starting at the center back. Place the edge of the cardboard tacking strip even with the line of stitches that secures the welt to the skirt. Place the tacks about 1 inch apart, in the center of the tacking strip. Stop when you reach the points at which the underneath pleat sections are to be added.

Position the underneath section so that it is centered between the two outer sections of the skirt; check that the hem length (drop) is even. Place a couple of tacks at the top of pleats to hold them in place. Bring the cardboard tacking strip over this section and tack it down. You are now tacking through the cardboard tacking strip (on the top), the underneath pleat section (in the middle), and the outer skirt section (on the bottom).

Once the skirt and pleats are tacked into place, fold the skirt down. Be sure that it is smooth where it meets the welt, and arrange the pleats neatly.

### Method 2

These instructions are for a skirt that is made in one piece.

If you are using a skirt that is sewn all in one piece, you have already added enough for each kickpleat (see page 30).

Fold back the allowances on each side to form the pleats, making sure that the seams are off-center and hidden under the pleats. Sew the welt to the top of the skirt and tack down or hand-sew the skirt as explained in Method 1.

## Dust Catcher

The bottom of any piece of furniture should be finished with either cambric or another plain fabric. If you are not applying a skirt, tack the fabric of the front arm panels to the underside of the furniture before attaching the dust catcher.

If you are adding a skirt, it is easier to cover the bottom before attaching the skirt. Tack the dust catcher all around the underside of the bottom rail, cutting out and folding under the fabric around the legs as necessary.

### Attaching Skirt

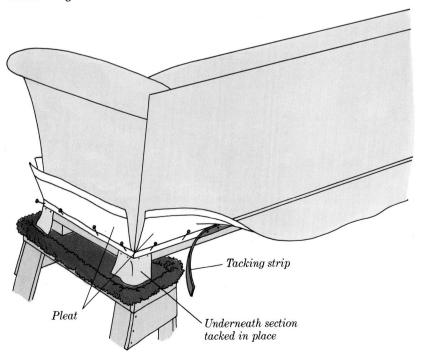

*Tacking strip*

*Pleat*

*Underneath section tacked in place*

# COVERING CUSHIONS & PILLOWS

T *he culminating step in most reupholstering projects is covering the boxed cushions that form an integral part of the piece, or making an assortment of throw pillows to complement the fabric of the finished piece. A couple of new techniques are introduced in this chapter—creating new cushions out of foam, and inserting zippers in boxing sections and in pillow covers. Also, a slightly different—and quicker—method for making welt is described.*

*With boxed cushions snugly in place and a few pillows thrown in for color and comfort, you can stand back and admire your handiwork.*

*Choosing fabric and trim for cushions and throw pillows is the time to let your imagination run riot. Be adventurous: Team stripes with polka dots and small patterns with large ones. Turn out square pillows, round ones, ruffled ones, and bolsters.*

# BOXED CUSHIONS

*C*ushions provide the finishing touch to your newly covered sofa or chair. The following directions for boxed cushions can be used not only for the seat and back cushions of an upholstered piece, but also for many types of chair seats that have either a foam base or a spring base.

If you are covering spring-base cushions that are in good shape, proceed. If they are worn or sag, consider substituting a foam base as described on this page.

## Foam Base

Foam tends to break down and crumble. If the foam in your cushions looks crumbly and old or does not bounce back when you press down on it, it is advisable to cut new foam for the seat and back cushions of the furniture.

Foam is available in varying thicknesses and lengths, and there are also different grades. Choosing a medium grade of foam is generally safe. You can feel the difference in quality when touching the various grades of foam. The better quality has a denser texture and does not give as easily when pressed. The thickness of the foam you buy should match your finished boxing measurement. Many suppliers of foam will cut pieces to the desired size or shape.

If you are covering a shaped cushion, use the cover as a pattern, carefully tracing the outline of the seams directly onto the foam with a felt-tipped pen. If the cushions are square or rectangular, simply measure out their shapes on the foam, using a ruler and felt-tipped pen.

When cutting a shaped foam cushion, cut ½ inch inside your marking lines if you plan to wrap the cushion in batting. (You must cut inside the lines because the pattern you used included seam allowances.) If you are not using batting, cut ¼ inch inside the lines, so that the foam will fill out the cover. You can always trim a little bit off, but it looks better when you have a tight, full fit.

Cut the foam with a serrated bread knife, an electric carving knife, or a hacksaw with a very fine blade. Starting at the farthest point away from you, make long, continuous cuts, drawing the knife toward you. Slice through the foam gradually, going just an inch or so deeper with each cut. Cutting in this manner keeps the edges of the foam smooth and even. Once the foam sections are all cut, they are ready to be wrapped in batting, if you choose.

## Batting-covered Foam

Foam is much more comfortable and looks much more elegant when it is wrapped. Batting takes away the sharp edges and provides a softer, fuller look; it also protects the foam.

Batting is sold in large rolls and is generally purchased by the yard. It can be found in most large fabric shops selling supplies for sewing projects for the home. Batting is basically stuffing in sheets, with a thin, synthetic fabric covering on one or both sides. This outer covering is sometimes stitched through to hold the batting together. The type without stitching is preferable, however, because the channels of stitching may show through your new cover if the fabric is light in weight.

Choose batting that is covered on one side only. If you are unable to find the unstitched type, it is easy enough to pull the stitching out.

Measure the batting to go around the top, bottom, and sides of the cushion and add a few extra inches to be turned in or sewn.

Wrap the batting around the piece of foam as shown in the illustration. Make sure that the folded portion is on the front edge of a seat cushion and the top edge of a back cushion. When sewing together, slightly overlap the open edges, pulling away a little of the stuffing to eliminate bulk. With needle and thread, and using long stitches, sew together until the foam is completely encased.

### Covering Foam with Batting

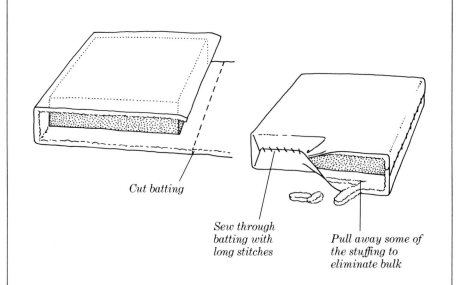

*Cut batting*

*Sew through batting with long stitches*

*Pull away some of the stuffing to eliminate bulk*

## Welt

If welt is to be used around the cushions, you can either make it separately (see page 28) or apply it directly to the cushions as you go along. This second method, which saves a little time, is discussed in this section. Measure the welt cord to go around the top and bottom of the cushions, adding a little extra that can be trimmed off once you are sure that the fit is accurate.

## Zippers

You will need a zipper foot and a zipper. Make sure that the zipper you buy is an appropriate weight for upholstery.

### Types

Zippers are sold ready-made, in certain standard sizes, or you can buy zipper tape by the inch in any length you need. When you buy by the inch, you are given the zipper pull separately and must attach it yourself.

Cutting your own length of zipper is usually preferable because you can get the precise length you need. If you make the opening a little short to accommodate a standard zipper size, it will be difficult to stuff the cushion into the cover.

### Measuring for Length

For seat cushions, measure the zipper so that it extends the length of the back of the cushion, goes around the corners, and wraps approximately 5½ inches down one side and 8½ inches down the pocket side.

For the back cushions, the zipper should go into boxing at the bottom of the cushion. Measure the zipper as described above except extend it 3½ inches on one side and 6½ for the pocket side. Before cutting the zipper, add 1 inch to these measurements. The zipper should be hidden when the cushions are in place.

## Cutting out the Boxing

The boxing depth should be the depth of the cushion plus seam allowances. The sections of boxing that will have a zipper inserted in them should be cut so that the top portion of the boxing is ½ inch larger than the lower portion. For example: If your finished boxing is to be 3 inches, the sections without the zipper should be 4 inches. For the sections with the zipper, the top portion with the overlap should be 3 inches and the lower section should be 2½ inches.

If possible, cut the boxing lengths in one piece. Allow enough to go across the front of the cushion and up the sides, leaving an extra 5½ inches on one side to provide the pocket that conceals the zipper pull. Center the pattern, if necessary.

If you need to attach a zipper pull, look for the arrows on the zipper tape; these indicate the direction in which the zipper closes. Put the pull on the end of the zipper and slide it in the direction of the arrows.

Place the zipper in the boxing so that the arrows point toward the side that will contain the pocket.

### *Estimating Length of Zipper*

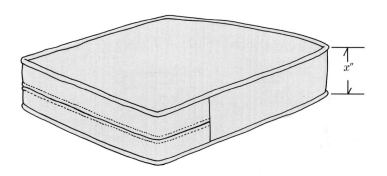

*Front boxing is x" deep. Cut piece x plus 1" (½" per seam allowance). Cut 2 pieces for boxing containing the zipper: 1 piece should be x", the other x minus ½"*

*Upper section*

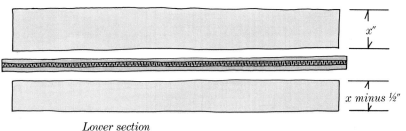

*Lower section*

## Attaching the Zipper

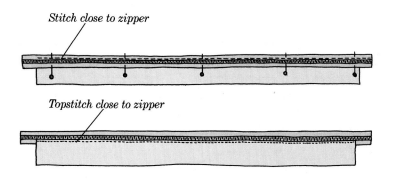

Stitch close to zipper

Topstitch close to zipper

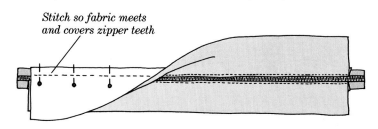

Stitch so fabric meets
and covers zipper teeth

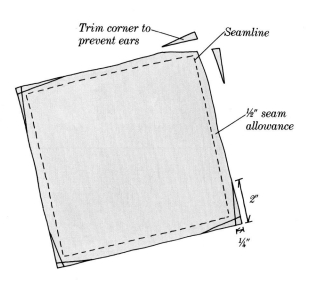

Trim corner to
prevent ears

Seamline

½" seam
allowance

2"

¼"

## Attaching the Zipper

With right sides together, pin the zipper onto the lower section of the boxing with the edges lined up. Using a zipper foot, sew the zipper to the boxing. Fold the zipper back to the right side. Topstitch fabric to the zipper tape with the foot guided by the edge of the zipper teeth.

Sew the top section of the boxing to the other side of the zipper in the same way. On this section, however, fold the fabric into a flap that covers the zipper teeth and meets the fabric of the bottom portion. Topstitch the fabric in place.

To attach the pull, open the zipper beginning at the tab end (the bottom), stopping about halfway. Thread the pull, widest part first, onto the bottom of the zipper. To make this easier, you can use pliers to pull a couple of teeth from the tab end of the zipper to get the threading started. Be careful not to cut or damage the zipper fabric. As you thread both sides of the zipper onto the pull, be sure to keep the end even. Once the pull is on, close the zipper halfway and heavily oversew both ends to prevent the pull from slipping off.

Shave off approximately ¼ inch on all corners of cushion covers, making a gradual cut about 2 inches long. This will prevent "ears" on finished cushions.

## Attaching the Welt

When attaching welt, start in the back of a seat cushion or the bottom of a back cushion leaving a tail approximately 4½ inches unattached.

When you reach a corner, stop approximately 1 inch away and make a diagonal cut through the welt fabric at the point where it will turn the corner. Stop sewing approximately 4½ inches before reaching the end.

Trim the welt cord so that ends will lie flat. Stitch fabric together with a bias seam. Trim seam and press it open. Line up all raw edges, and sew this last section onto the cushion.

# Attaching Welt

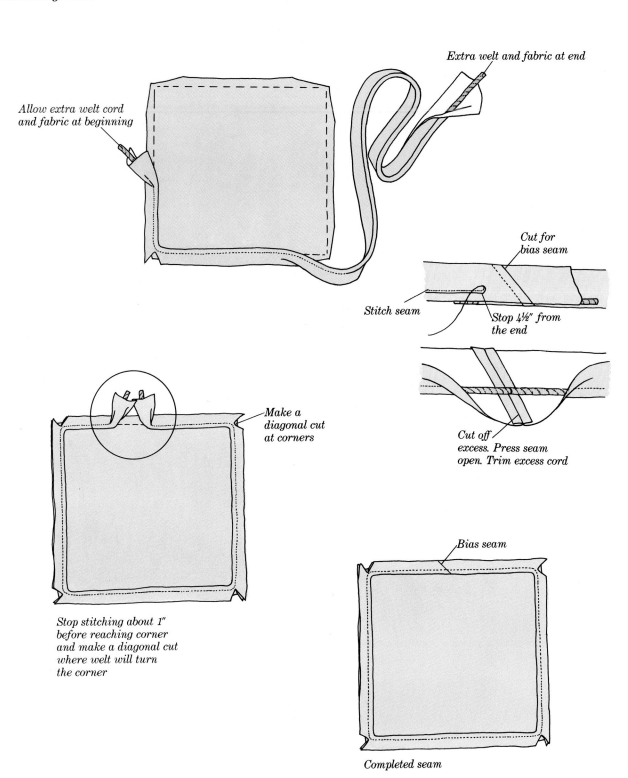

Extra welt and fabric at end

Allow extra welt cord and fabric at beginning

Cut for bias seam

Stitch seam

Stop 4½" from the end

Cut off excess. Press seam open. Trim excess cord

Make a diagonal cut at corners

Stop stitching about 1" before reaching corner and make a diagonal cut where welt will turn the corner

Bias seam

Completed seam

## Attaching Boxing Sections

Start stitching 8" from corner

Fit and ease around corners

Back, bottom corner

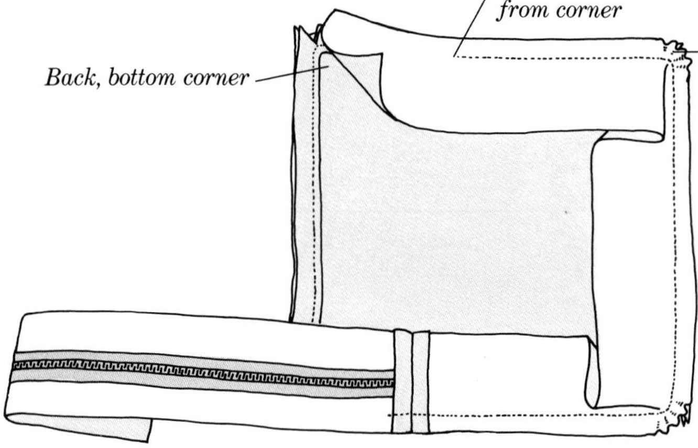

1. Stitch piece containing zipper to boxing with right sides together

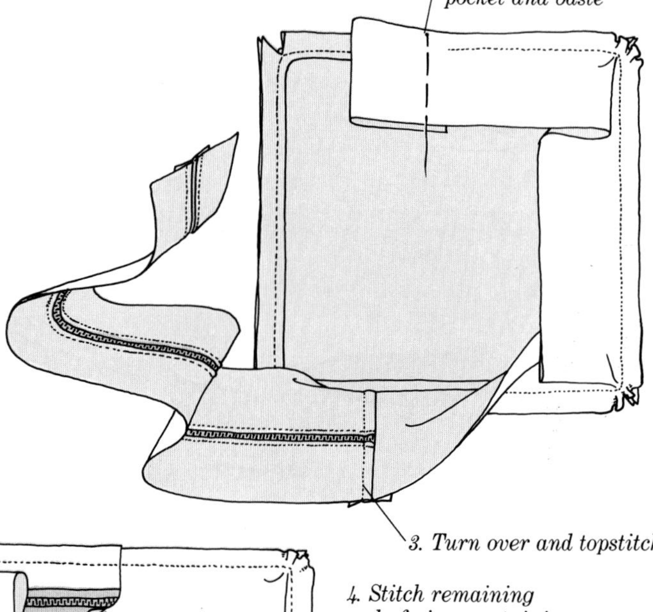

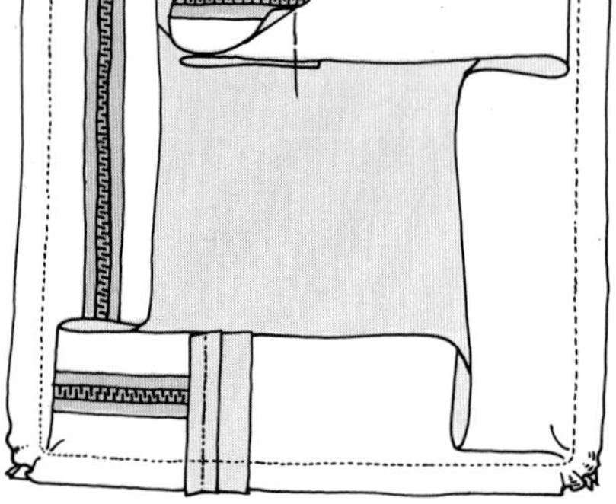

2. Fold under for pocket and baste

3. Turn over and topstitch

4. Stitch remaining end of piece containing zipper over pocket. Open zipper before sewing other side of cover to boxing

## Attaching Boxing Sections

If the front and side boxing was cut in one piece, proceed from the back corner after checking that pattern on front edge will match top and bottom sections. Start stitching 8 inches away from this corner, continuing across the front and up the second side, stopping 4½ inches short of the other back corner.

Position the zippered section of boxing as shown in the illustration. Starting at the tab end of the zipper, sew it to the boxing, right sides together. Turn over and topstitch on the front side, taking care not to break the machine needle when sewing over the zipper teeth.

Now sew the zippered section to the cushion section. Begin sewing where the seam for the front boxing ended. Fit and ease around the corners, and stop sewing approximately 3 inches before you reach the end.

Stitch the two remaining ends of the boxing together. Fold the pocket as shown in the illustration. Pin or baste the pocket into position and complete the sewing.

Before you begin sewing the other side of the cushion to the boxing, open the zipper partway. This will allow you to turn the cushion cover right side out when you have finished sewing. Once you have done this, pin the other side of the cushion to the boxing, and sew the two together.

## Stuffing the Cover

If cushion is foam or foam wrapped in batting, fold it in half and stuff it as far as possible inside the cover and then unfold it. Push corners of cushion into corners of cover, making sure that the edges of the welt are pushed down evenly all around the inside. As you close the zipper make sure that the batting, if there is any, does not get stuck in the zipper teeth.

If using a spring cushion, carefully slide it in, easing on the cover one side at a time.

# THROW PILLOWS

*Decorative cushions and throw pillows are an important addition to any scheme. They are fast, easy, and fun to make, and they are also one of those finishing touches that make a room cozy, add splashes of color, and pull together colors and textures for a harmonious look.*

Many shapes and styles are fashionable nowadays, but often the simplest square pillow (a knife-edge) is the most successful. This type can be made in an assortment of sizes to be scattered on a sofa or window seat. You can use the same fabric for all of the pillows, or blend hues of plain-colored fabrics. You can also mix and match patterns. This solution is especially effective if the room is fairly plain otherwise.

## Stuffing

If you wish to make old cushions or pillows a little fuller or larger before recovering them, wrap them in batting as described in covering foam seats (see page 66). If you are using the batting with a covering on one side, the old pillows can be wrapped and hand-stitched to produce whatever size or fullness you wish by simply adding more layers. Whether using old pillow forms or selecting new ones, always choose ones that are a little larger than the size of the finished cover.

Remember when planning the size of the cover that, once stuffed, the pillow will measure about 2 inches less than the flat cover.

## Synthetic Fillers

When starting from scratch, you have a large choice of pillow forms available at sewing supply stores.

The least expensive forms are filled with shredded foam, which tends to be lumpy unless it is covered with a heavy fabric. It does not make up into a soft or comfortable pillow. If you already own this type of pillow and plan to recover it, wrap it in batting first; the end results will be far more pleasing.

Polyester fiberfill, covered in a mesh of thin synthetic fabric or sometimes muslin, is a medium-priced filler. With this type of form, be sure that all of the corners are fully stuffed. Work carefully. The thin cover can tear easily and if all of the stuffing gets pushed into the center, it can be difficult to redistribute it.

## Natural Fillers

Kapok fillers covered in a fire-retardant heavy cotton hold their shape beautifully over a long period of time and are an excellent choice. With heavy use, they may pack down after a while but a good beating will fluff them up. Although rather expensive, they are well worth the investment.

Down pillows are truly wonderful. They are lightweight, full, luxuriously comfortable, and they retain their shape. Their one disadvantage is that they are very expensive. Some places will make down pillows to size. Or you can make your own by shaking down old, limp featherbed pillows into squares, doing a couple of rows of machine-stitching, then cutting off the excess pillow fabric. From a tired, shapeless old pillow, you now have a fat and full pillow form.

*Rather than making one large pillow to put in the corner of a sofa, think about making several small ones. This way you can use a variety of fabrics that coordinate with all the other color and pattern elements in your room.*

## Cutting

When cutting pillow sections for a square or knife-edge pillow, with or without a welt, measure the squares for the top and bottom to include a ¾-inch (rather than the usual ½-inch) seam allowance. The additional allowance will make inserting the zipper easier, especially if you decide to use a lapped application.

Cut the front and back sections together, unless you have a pattern to center, in which case cut them separately. Approximately 2 inches from each side of the corners, starting ¼ inch down, shave away a small wedge of fabric. This will prevent the finished cover from having "ears," or corners that are too sharply pointed.

Choose a zipper roughly 3 inches shorter than the length of the side that you are placing it in.

For a simple cover without a welt or ruffle, the zipper is the first step. It is inserted before any of the other seams are sewn up. There are two application techniques, centered and lapped, the centered version being the easiest. For either version, first place the two pieces of fabric right sides together and sew up the seam. Use machine basting stitches through the section where the zipper will be, and regular stitches at the beginning and end. Press open the seam.

### Centered Application

With the front and back of the pillow opened out flat, place zipper right side down, centering teeth on the seam line. Baste. Using the zipper foot, sew zipper following the guideline on the tape. Oversew top and bottom for additional strength.

On the right side of the cover, open the basting stitches using a seam ripper or small scissors.

Next sew the other three sides of the cushion. Remember that the zipper should be opened so that the cover can be turned right side out once completed.

### Lapped Application

Open zipper and place face down on the extended seam allowance with the zipper teeth on the seam line. Using the zipper foot, machine-baste from bottom up, following the guideline on the tape. Close zipper and turn face up. Smooth fabric away from zipper, and starting from the bottom, topstitch through the folded seam allowance.

Spread the cover flat, with zipper now face down on the other seam allowance. Turn pull tab up. Stitch across bottom and up the other side of zipper, oversewing the top. Turn to right side and remove basting stitches. Open zipper, then sew remaining three sides of the cover.

### Welt

If you are adding welt to the cover, baste covered welting cord on the right side of the fabric on the cover front, with edges lined up and corners clipped.

With right sides together, sew the portion of the seam where zipper begins and ends, using a zipper foot and keeping stitches close to welting. Starting with the seam allowance that has the attached welt, place zipper face down with teeth lined up close to welt. Sew through all the thicknesses, using zipper tape as a guideline.

Open the front and back cover sections and sew remaining zipper into place.

Sew remaining three sides together, still using the zipper foot and keeping it close to the edge of the welt. Trim corners to reduce bulk, and turn right side out.

## Boxed Cushion for a Window Seat

In making a window seat, the first step is to decide on the depth of foam you want to use. Consider the height of the window seat itself, and then whether comfort requires just a 1-inch foam pad or something plushier, perhaps a 2- or 3-inch piece of foam wrapped in batting. The next step is to make a pattern for the cushion if the seat is an irregular shape.

To do this, tape together sheets of kraft paper a little larger than the area you are tracing. Place the paper on the seat and carefully follow the shape with a felt-tip pen or a pencil.

After cutting out the pattern, place it directly on the foam and again mark the outline with a felt-tipped pen. Directions for cutting the foam are on page 66. Using the same pattern for your fabric cover, add the boxing amount by measuring half the depth of the foam and then adding this to all of the sides, plus the seam allowances.

If you plan to make the cover with separate boxing, add only the seam allowance to the pattern, then cut the boxing sections according to the depth of the foam, adding seam allowances.

The first style of cover is suitable if the cushion is perfectly rectangular. If the window seat is angled and you are dealing with a wedge shape with pointed corners, you will achieve a better fit by using separate boxing. With this second style of cover, when you cut the fabric on an angle you will be creating a bias cut, so be sure to baste carefully when you sew sections together or add welting. Otherwise the cover may stretch or pucker.

If the cover fabric has a pattern that cannot be railroaded or made in one continuous piece, make the window seat out of separate sections. The number and size of cushions will depend on the length of the seat and on how many times the width of the pattern you wish to center will fit. Simply divide the front length by the number of cushions you decide on, and cut the pattern with the shaping accordingly. Always remember to add boxing and seam allowances.

Sew the cover according to the directions for the particular style, wrap the foam in batting, place stuffing in the cover, and place cushions on the seat. Pile on loads of matching pillows to create a most inviting seating area.

## Ruffled Throw Pillow

For a prettier and more feminine look, you may wish to add a ruffle to your throw pillow. This is particularly suitable for a pillow that will be tossed onto a bed or in the corner of a chintz-covered sofa.

If you wish to add a ruffle, there are several ways to close the case without using a zipper.

### Method 1

The first method is to cut the cushion back and front to the size needed, measure the distance all around, and cut ruffle strips equalling three times this measurement. Depending on the pattern of your fabric, the strips may be cut across the width and seamed together. Trim close to the stitches and press the seam open to prevent bulk. Or they may be taken from the length, in which case you should cut off the selvage.

For a 2-inch ruffle, cut the strips 5 inches wide. Sew all of the strips together so that they form a circle, fold the width evenly in half, and press in a sharp fold.

Using the longest basting stitch on your machine, sew two rows of stitches a little short of the ½-inch seam allowance. Gently gather the ruffle, little by little, so that the

stitches do not break. Work until you have reached the finished measurement needed for the perimeter of the cushion and all gathers are evenly distributed.

With the ruffle facing into the center of the pillow front and all raw edges lined up, pin or baste into position. Place the back on top and pin or baste this into position also. Start sewing all of these pieces together at the bottom of the pillow, a couple of inches from the outer corners. Sew all the way around until you reach the bottom again, then continue sewing for another couple of inches. Press the bottom seam allowances that have not been stitched. Clip the corners and turn the cover right side out. After stuffing the pillow, hand-sew the closure together with blind stitches along the pressed seam allowance line.

### Method 2

Another way to close this type of cushion is to cut the front section in one piece but the back in two pieces. The back should measure the same as the front plus 5 inches. Cut in half. Sew the ruffle and position it on the front section of the pillow in the same way as described above.

Turn in the two center back seams, taking ¼ inch twice so that there are no raw edges; topstitch. Place the back sections on the pillow and ruffle so that the center seams are overlapping and all the outside raw edges are even. Sew all sections together, then turn right side out. You now have a center overlap into which you can place the pillow form one side at a time.

## Flanged Pillow

Flanged pillows, like ruffled pillows, have an extended outer border, but the flange is flat and tailored.

To the dimensions of the inner pillow form, add the depth of the flange you wish. This is usually 2 to 3 inches, but in any case should be propor-

tional to the size of the pillow you are making. Add this amount, plus the seam allowances, to all of the sides. When cutting the back, add 5 inches and cut in half, through the center, from top to bottom. Turn in and sew ¼ inch twice down the center pieces.

Place the front and back sections together, with all raw edges lined up and the overlapping section in the center back. Stitch all four edges, clip the corners, turn right side out, and press. Measure and mark the depth of the flange carefully with chalk. Topstitch along these lines, brushing off chalk marks as you go. The pillow can be filled in the back in the same manner as the ruffled pillow.

## Instant Throw Pillow

This is a wonderfully quick way to make a flanged pillow for either a bed or a sofa, without a zipper, envelope closure, or hand-sewing. All of the work is done on the sewing machine following some careful measuring and aided by some crisp pressing and Velcro fastening tape.

Measure the pillow form and add 9½ inches to your measurements. Cut two pieces of fabric to these measurements.

Working with the front side of the fabric face down, fold over ½ inch on all sides and press with an iron. Then fold down 4 inches on all sides, making envelope-style folds at each corner. Iron firmly in place.

Measure and cut four pieces of Velcro fastening tape to fit around bottom edges of fold. Miter-cut tape so corners will fit together neatly. Stitch Velcro fastening tape in place.

Repeat the same steps on second pillow section. Place pillow form in the center and seal front and back together with the Velcro.

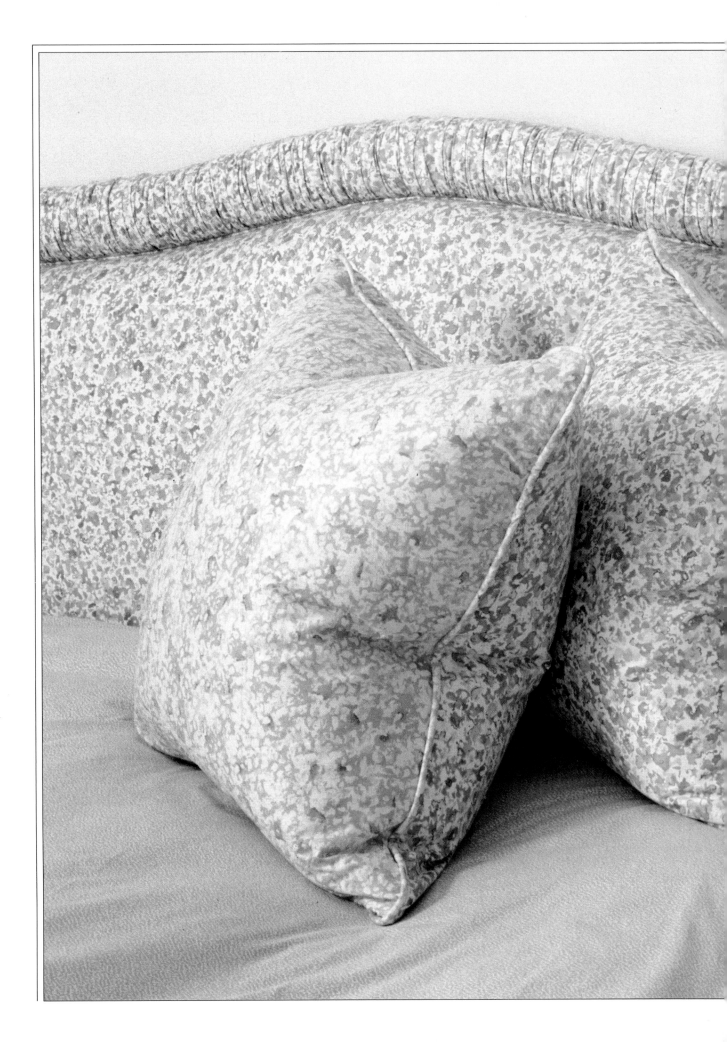

# SPECIAL PROJECTS

In this section the meaning of upholstery is stretched to embrace an imaginative group of ideas for softening or enlivening the surfaces of your home with fabric coverings. Create a coordinated bedroom with a padded headboard, an upholstered base, and a matching quilt cover. Fashion a display of multicolored and textured throw pillows for a window seat or bed.

The following suggestions are intended to encourage you to consider upholstery when you are looking for a decorating solution—or just a fun project. The basic upholstery techniques described earlier apply here as well.

*A luxuriously soft headboard is just one of the special upholstery projects that appear on the following pages. To make this (or a variation on this theme), see page 77.*

# FITTED BED COVERS

**F**itted bed covers lie flat on a bed, with the corners of one end fitted at the bottom of the mattress and the other end, unfitted, extending a little beyond the top of the mattress. The sides are not tucked under but hang just below the mattress. With this style of cover, you should add pillow cases, as a pillow allowance would disrupt the close fitting.

## Materials

The easiest way to make a fitted bed cover is by using sheets, which don't need extra seams. The sheet you choose must be large enough to cover the width of the bed plus a blanket allowance of approximately 4 inches, plus the depth of the mattress on both sides, plus seam allowances. The sheet's length should be the length of the bed, plus the 4-inch blanket allowance, plus the depth of the mattress at the bottom only, plus seam allowances.

You will need a lining of the same dimensions. This can be an additional sheet, but make sure that the lining color does not show through.

If you are using 54-inch fabric, you will need two lengths to cover a double bed. Center one length on the bed, divide the second length in half, and sew to the two sides of the first length. You must match patterns; a consideration you should remember when buying the fabric.

## Making the Cover

To make the cover, place fabric and lining right sides together and sew around all the edges, leaving roughly 24 inches open at bottom for turning case right side out. Trim corners. Turn case right side out and press seams.

Place cover on bed, face down, and position it so that all sides with their allowances are even. At each bottom corner, take up excess fabric until you have an even fit, and pin together. Mark or baste this line and sew. Cut off excess, and press open the seam. Turn cover right side up and fit onto bed, making sure that corners fit snugly.

If you are making a bed cover for a daybed, add an additional mattress and seam allowance for both bottom and top when you are estimating the yardage. Then finish top corners as you did the two bottom ones.

If desired, add trim around edges.

*A fitted bed cover is an extremely easy project that can be made out of sheets.*

# HEADBOARDS

*G*ive your bedroom a real lift by upholstering the headboard to match or contrast the bed cover.

You will need a sheet of plywood cut to size, batting, a staple gun, and fabric. The plywood should be as wide as the outside measurement of the bed frame and as high as you want the finished headboard to be.

## Making the Cover

First cover the front side. Attach sheets of batting to front of plywood, extending batting 4 inches around to the back. Staple batting to back every 2 inches, being sure that all outer edges are smooth and even.

Measure and cut fabric by laying it on headboard. Allow an extra 6 to 8 inches all around. Before stapling, check that your fabric or design is positioned straight on the rectangle. Put four staples in center of each side to hold fabric in place. Then continue working from side to side, moving away from center and stapling every 2 inches. Leave 4 inches unstapled at each corner so that you can finish corners with pleats or hospital folds; then staple them into place.

To cover the back side, cut a piece of fabric the size of the headboard. Starting at center of each side again, repeat stapling, tucking edges under as you go. Once completed, you may cover staples with a grosgrain ribbon, applied with glue.

An alternative method (one that does not require a staple gun) is to make a fitted case and pull it over the entire headboard. Cut two pieces of fabric to dimensions of headboard, with allowances for batting width and seams. Sew together sides and top, slightly curving corners because batting will prevent them from being square. Ease case over wood and batting, covering headboard completely. Finish cover by turning under raw edge at bottom and hand-sewing fabric to batting.

## Edging

Just covering the front and back will result in a neat, tailored look. However, if you want a more decorative look, there are many ways to edge the headboard.

To achieve the effect shown here, tightly roll a piece of batting lengthwise and cover it as you would welt cord (see page 28). Gather the cover slightly to achieve a gathered look.

## Attaching the Headboard

To hold the headboard in position, either bolt it to the bed frame or box spring, or attach it to the wall behind the bed.

*Upholstering a headboard gives you a soft surface against which to recline.*

# BED BASES

**W**hether your mattress is supported by a box spring or a wood base, you can cover it to coordinate or contrast the headboard and bed cover.

## Covering a Box Spring

If you plan to use a bed sheet as your cover, be sure that it is thick enough to obscure any design and color on the box spring. Choose a size that is large enough to cover the top and sides of the box spring plus an extra 4 to 6 inches for attaching it to the underside.

If you are concerned about the color or pattern on the box spring showing through, or if you want a softer look, wrap box spring with batting before covering it. Use a strip of batting wide enough to cover sides, plus extend 4 to 6 inches over the top as well as the same amount underneath the box spring. Using a semi-circular upholstery needle and long stitches, attach batting to top of box spring. Staple it to the underside.

If using a decorating fabric, you will need two lengths seamed together. The seam at the bottom of the bed will be visible, therefore patterned fabric should be matched.

Spread sheet or fabric over top of box spring. On the underside, place one tack or staple in the center of each of the four sides. Working on one side at a time, staple fabric in place, working out towards corners.

At the corners, make either crisp pleats or small folds. Staple them in place and trim off all excess fabric.

After it is upholstered, you can replace the box spring on a bed frame. However, an attractive touch is to support the box spring on upholstered legs (see page 83).

## Covering a Wood Base

If you prefer to sleep on a firmer bed, you may wish to buy or make and then cover a wood base.

There are many different types of bases available; on some, the mattress fits within the frame. The one shown opposite consists of a recessed frame topped by a sheet of plywood the same size as the mattress.

After making the frame, glue on batting and upholster the base as described above.

*Above: Create a romantic bedroom by covering the box spring with a ruffled skirt and adding posts draped with matching fabric.*
*Opposite: By upholstering a simple wood frame and a piece of plywood you can fashion an elegant bed base.*

# FUTON & QUILT COVERS

**B**oth of these covers are simply large sacks with a zipper or Velcro fastening tape sewn in one side to make it easy to remove.

Sheets make ideal covers because they do not need to be seamed and because they will stand up to repeated laundering. You might consider using flannel sheets; they now come in wonderful colors and patterns and they are soft and warm.

## Making a Futon Cover

You will need two pieces of fabric the size of your futon, plus half the depth of the stuffing, plus a seam allowance. (If you plan to use fastening tape for the closure, add an extra 1-inch seam allowance to both pieces along the edge where you plan to attach it.)

### Inserting the Closure

The closure can be placed so that it is centered down the length of the underneath section, but this means extra seams. The following instructions are for placing it in one of the side seams. This works just as well although the closure will show slightly.

*Using a zipper.* With right sides of the fabric together, baste the side of the cover in which the zipper will be placed. The zipper should extend the entire length minus approximately 5 inches at each end. Proceed with the directions for inserting a lapped zipper (see page 68).

*Using Velcro fastening tape.* On both top and bottom cover sections, fold cut edge under, then press a 1-inch seam down the length of the side in which the tape will be sewn. Cut tape to length: It should extend the entire length minus approximately 5 inches at each end.

Separate the pieces of fastening tape and stitch one to each cover section. Press pieces of tape together, and machine- or hand-stitch the seam above and below the closure.

### Seaming the Cover

Pull open a few inches of the closure and, with right sides together, sew the remaining three sides. Box the corners the depth of stuffing (see page 67). Turn cover right side out, iron it, and insert the futon.

## Making a Quilt Cover

If you are making a quilt cover to match, follow directions for making the futon cover but place the closure along the bottom end and omit the boxed corners.

When sewing the top and bottom sections together, slightly round the corners to prevent "ears." To give your quilt cover a professional touch, you might wish to add matching or contrasting welt (see page 28).

Another special touch is to add ties: Thread ribbon through a needle with a large eye and make one small stitch completely through quilt so that both ends of ribbon will be on top section of the cover. Tie ends in a bow. Quilt the cover in the pattern of your choice using as many ties as you wish. However, remember that it will be necessary to remove these ties in order to launder the cover.

**Above:** *Covering the mattress makes a guest bed look more like a sofa.*
**Opposite:** *Charmingly covered futons make even the floor look invitingly soft.*

# FABRIC-COVERED TABLES

You can turn a simple rectangular table into a decorative dressing table or end table by adding some padding and an interesting fabric. Consider this kind of upholstery to add a touch of glamor to a teenager's room—or to your own.

To start your project, measure the table as follows, and cut out your pieces of fabric. To all measurements, add ½ inch for a seam allowance and an extra ¼ inch to allow for the padding—¾ inch in all.

Measure the top of the table. If the wood is no more than 1½ inches thick, seam allowance will be sufficient to create a neat edge. If it is thicker, measure depth and cut a separate strip for boxing. Do this in four sections, making seams at each corner to give a close fit. Then measure length of legs, allowing extra fabric for stapling at top and for wrapping under and attaching to bottom of legs. Cut out sections.

## Covering the Legs

Turn table upside down and wrap batting around so that it encases a whole leg, with seam ending up on inside corner edge. Pin along seam to hold batting in place. Staple at top and bottom and hand-sew seam to secure batting. Repeat on all legs.

Wrap fabric tightly over batting with seam ending up in same place. Pin all along seam.

Staple fabric at very top of leg, or underneath if your table design will allow. At bottom of leg, staple fabric underneath where it can't be seen, making small tight pleats at corners. Hand-sew seam using small blind stitches.

## Covering the Tabletop

Place a layer of padding over top of table, wrapping it around to the underside. Clip corners in order to avoid bulk. The corners will retain their shape better if you hand-sew the batting around them.

Place fabric over batting. Clip and pleat at corners and staple to underside of tabletop. Stitch fabric where top and leg join, using small blind stitches.

## Adding the Skirt

The table will now look wonderful just as it is, but if you wish to turn it into a full-fledged dressing table, proceed as follows.

Measure all four sides of the tabletop and multiply total by three. Cut fabric to that measurement, adding seam allowance. The depth of panels should be the length of tabletop, plus ½ inch for hem, if you are adding lining, or 3 inches if you are not. Add 4 inches to top.

If you are making the skirt without a lining, seam all pieces together. Turn in a ½-inch seam allowance and 2½-inch hem. Stitch.

At top, turn in a ½-inch seam allowance and press. Fold down 3½ inches and press. Then sew on curtain tape to make gathering easier. Starting ¾ inch down, line up 1 inch of curtain tape with two cords running through it. Sew this along edges on both sides, leaving openings at center back.

Start the next gathering tape ¾ inch down and stitch with the ½-inch seam allowance folded under. Gather fabric, distributing evenly. Pin fabric around tabletop, with ¾ inch of ruffle extending above top. Adjust cords and gathers. Tie cords tightly in back and cut away excess.

Hand-stitch skirt to table, making sure that stitches don't show.

You can also line the skirt, to give it weight and, if you're using finer fabric, to give the whole table a fuller look. First sew panels of skirt fabric together, then sew panels of lining together. Seam both sets of panels all around bottom, using the ½-inch seam allowance. Press seam.

Fold over the double thickness of fabric at top, turning in the ½-inch seam allowance and 3½-inch fold. Press. Continue handling skirt and lining as one piece, and finish skirt as described above.

An attractive way to finish the table is by laying a piece of glass cut to size inside the ruffled border of the tabletop. Finally, you can center an ornate, free-standing mirror on the glass to complete the dressing-room look.

## Alternative Covers

Maybe you wish to cover a table in a coordinating or contrasting fabric, but don't wish to do the work involved in upholstering the legs and top. If this is the case, there are other covers you can make.

The simplest method, and one that is very fashionable, is to wrap the table in fabric. Tie the wrap to the table with ribbon, welting that matches other upholstered furniture, or with rope or cord.

To cover a round-topped table, make a circular cloth and drape it over the top. The diameter of the cloth should be the diameter of the tabletop, plus the distance from tabletop to floor times two, plus an allowance for a hem. If the resulting measurement is more than the width of your fabric, cut the cloth in two pieces and allow a little extra to seam pieces together.

# UPHOLSTERED FEET

For a special decorator touch, consider covering the feet on pieces of furniture. Many pieces already have wood feet or blocks. If yours does not, this might be an attractive alternative to a metal bed frame or a way to raise a sofa that is uncomfortably low.

## Making the Feet

If your furniture does not have feet, make them out of blocks of wood. Round feet can be made by cutting 4-inch lengths of 4x4 and wrapping the cubes with batting. Unusual effects can be achieved by stacking rectangles in different lengths, or (on lighter pieces) you can make interesting legs out of banister rail.

## Covering the Feet

There is no particular method for covering wood blocks. The only principle is to do the job as neatly as possible and the make sure that the edges and the fold are on the two faces that will not show—the ones that make contact with the floor and with the underside of the piece of furniture.

Pleats and gathers can be stitched before wrapping the blocks. Batting, to soften the look, can be either glued to the block or stitched to the fabric. Use whichever method results in the neatest look.

**Above:** *Even though the decking and the arms are separate sections, note the straightness of the stripes and how well the pieces are matched.*
**Left:** *If a sofa is a little low, raise it by placing it on upholstered blocks of wood.*

# SEAT INSERTS

**O**n many dining chairs, the upholstered seat is a separate piece that is dropped in place and screwed to the frame.

Once this piece is removed, it is a simple job to replace both the cover and the padding.

## Replacing the Seat

Turn the chair over and release the seat from the frame. This may require removing screws, nails, or pegs driven through corner blocks or into the frame. Remove the old cover that is usually stapled or tacked to the seat piece. If the padding is lumpy, remove and replace it. Cut the padding slightly smaller than the seat to make sure that the newly covered seat will still fit the frame, and to get a smooth curve on all sides. Hold padding in place with a couple of dabs of glue.

Using the old cover as a pattern, cut out fabric; take care to carefully center any pattern. Center fabric over padding on the seat and stretch it around to underside. Temporarily attach with one tack or staple on each side. Check positioning, then permanently tack or staple one side, stopping a little short of each corner. Attach the opposite side in the same way, pulling the fabric a little as you work. Attach the remaining two sides.

The corners require care to avoid bulky pleats. Grip one corner of the fabric and pull it firmly to the underside of the seat, placing a tack or staple near the point. Make diagonal cuts on either side of the point, stopping about ¾ of an inch from the corner of the seat. You now have a slightly tapered strip anchored down by the tack or staple. On each side of this strip, make a cut at right angles to the first cut to remove excess fabric. Fold side pieces into a neat corner and tack or staple in place. Screw newly covered seat to the frame.

## Replacing the Back

Unlike the underside of the seat, the back side of a seat back will be visible. Therefore both sides must look neat. You can upholster the back first and cover raw edges with padding and front panel. Or you can cover the front first, attach the back panel, and cover the join with braid or decorative tacks. The choice depends on the chair frame and the look you wish to achieve.

Apply padding and fabric as described in Replacing the Seat. If the frame will cover the join, fold under raw edges of fabric and staple in place. If it will not, conceal join with braid or decorative tacks or turn under raw edges and hand-stitch around all four edges.

## Making a Seat

If you own a chair with a broken cane insert, consider upholstering it rather than recaning.

After removing the cane bead that runs around the caned section the seat can be removed and covered as described above. Or you will discover that the cane is woven through holes in the frame, in which case you will need to make a seat.

If the caning holes were drilled in a routed groove, use the groove to support a new seat cut out of ½-inch plywood. For strength, fill caning holes before insetting seat.

If there is no groove, either attach support rails to the underside of the frame or cut the plywood seat slightly larger than the opening in the frame.

**Above:** *When using a striped fabric, make sure to line up the stripes on the back with those on the seat.*
**Opposite:** *Chair seats are upholstered in a fabric that matches the upholstered walls.*

# UPHOLSTERED WALLS

**W**hether covered in cotton duck or raw silk, upholstered walls can be very dramatic. The fabric used on the walls can also be made into rich full drapes or roman shades.

Aside from the drama, there are many practical advantages to upholstering walls. The soft, luxurious look and feel of fabric over batting cannot be duplicated by any other material. This decorative treatment will conceal dated wallcovering, dark paneling, or badly cracked walls without your having to strip, spackle, resurface, sand, and paint or wallpaper. An added bonus is that an upholstered wall provides both heat insulation and soundproofing.

Almost any room can be upholstered, but it is recommended that you start with a space that does not have too many windows, doors, or tricky alcoves. It is also better to choose a pattern without a large repeat or one that requires exact matching.

The only places where upholstered walls are not recommended are a bathroom or any room that tends to be damp. If you do not have good extractor fans or ventilation, the fabric will retain moisture and is likely to mildew. In other rooms, the only care needed for fabric-covered walls is occasional light vacuuming or dusting with a soft broom.

## Fabric
It is preferable to buy yardage rather than to use sheets. Your choice is much broader and the quality of the printing is better, especially when it comes to matching a pattern.

Use 54-inch-wide fabric that has a tight weave and will not stretch when you apply tension. For a first installation, it is a good idea to stay away from fabrics that are heavy or have patterns that will be hard to match.

To estimate the amount of fabric needed, measure the wall area to be covered, ignoring windows and doors. Divide the total wall area by the area that can be covered by one 54-inch width hanging from ceiling to floor. The result will be the number of panels you will need. Add the pattern repeat measurement plus a little extra for turning under raw edges; then multiply this total length by the number of panels to arrive at the yardage needed.

*Welt.* If you plan to use double welt to conceal staples, estimate fabric needs by allowing 1½ yards of 54-inch-wide fabric for approximately 25 yards of double welt.

*Polyester batting.* If possible, buy batting that is 54 inches wide. If this width is not available, purchase the widest possible.

The thickness depends on the look you wish to achieve. Generally, ¾-inch-deep batting is used, but you may find that ½ inch is sufficient for your needs. Estimate the amount by calculating the number of panels in the same way as you estimated fabric (see above), but omitting the extra amounts for pattern repeat and turning under edges.

## Means of Attachment
Batting and fabric are stapled directly to the wall. There are very few walls that will not accept staples, but you should test this out before launching into the project.

If you do have a wall that will not accept staples, you can attach a framework of wood furring strips. These should not be more than ½ inch thick (less if possible). The strips must extend around the ceiling, baseboard, down each side of a corner, and all around a doorway or window. In other words, anywhere you need to attach the fabric there must be a

furring strip into which you can staple. Explain the stapling problem to a salesperson at your local lumberyard or hardware store and ask what type of fastener to use. Attach furring strips to the wall using the recommended fastener.

Proceed by attaching batting and fabric as described below, stapling either into the furring strips or directly into the wall.

Whichever way the fabric is attached, there will be visible staples all around the room. These can be covered with strips of molding or, as is often the case with professional installations, with double welt made from matching fabric. The welt is glued on after the walls are upholstered.

## Preparation
First remove light plates and any obstacles from the wall to be covered.

Fabric panels are sewn together so that each wall is covered in a single "sheet" of fabric. These sheets meet, slightly overlapping, at each corner of the room. As the pattern will be most noticeable in areas high on the wall, do your matching at the top of each panel. Extra inches at the bottom can be trimmed later.

Cut out all panels, then sew them together for each wall you are covering. Place panels face together and, as you sew them, keep checking to be sure that the pattern is matched perfectly. When panels are joined, press open seams.

## Attaching Batting
Staple batting to walls or furring strips, stopping about 1 inch short of ceiling, baseboard, corners, windows, doors, or any other area that

*Upholstering the walls is a practical way to cover a multitude of sins as well as to insulate and soundproof. It is also a decorative way to coordinate furnishings.*

*Imitate a chair rail molding by attaching fabric trim part way up an upholstered wall. Note how the fabric used matches the tieback on the drape.*

## Attaching Fabric

Temporarily pin fabric sheet along the top. Fold raw edge under and start stapling in the center, working to the outside. Make sure sheet lies flat.

Once fabric is attached at the top, pin it to the wall and cut out necessary shapes around doors and windows. Staple the sides, overlapping them at any corner where another sheet of fabric will meet.

Then, staple the bottom by starting in the center and working out toward the corners. (It is easier to get a good grip and apply tension to the fabric if you do not turn under the raw edge at the bottom. The edge can be covered with baseboard molding.) When stapled, trim off excess at the bottom. Use a single-edge razor blade and trim as close to the staples as possible.

Now all of the staples must be covered. If you are using molding, cut it (mitering the corners) and paint the pieces before attaching them. When paint is dry, nail molding in place, countersink finishing nails, and touch up with paint.

## Adding Welt Trim

To make double welt, cut bias strips 2¾ inches wide. Seam them together as described on page 29. With fabric face down, center a length of welt cord and fold fabric in half. On top of folded fabric, place second cord next to first piece, then fold fabric back to cover. With a sewing machine, stitch the full length of the strip. Center stitching line between the two cords. Trim away any excess fabric.

Glue the welt over all stapled edges. At corners, push apart the two cords and hammer a finishing nail between them. Do the same on large runs or wherever you think that glue is not strong enough to hold the welt securely in place.

will be finished with molding or welt.

To make batting seams even and smooth, butt panels together and pin temporarily in place. Gently pull back the top layers before stapling the panel to the wall. After doing this on both edges of adjacent panels, smooth top layers back in place.

When batting is attached, trim around windows, doors, and light fixtures. Start in the center and work outward. Leave about 1 inch of wall space in areas where molding or welt will be applied.

# DIRECTOR'S CHAIR COVERS

**D**ue to the reasonable price, the comfort it offers, and the fact it can be folded and put away, the director's chair has become a standard in game rooms, first apartments, and student dorms.

With a small amount of fabric and effort, graduates can turn these standards into decorator specials by replacing the plain-colored covers with ones that coordinate with a tablecloth. Or, in a bedroom, chair covers can match the sheets or drapes.

Cutting out the fabric is easy. Both the back and seat covers are merely rectangles with side seams. The back cover slips over the chair rails. On the seat, dowels slip into the seams to hold the fabric in place. Use the old cover as a guide, making allowances for the fact that the existing cover may have stretched. Or measure the distance from side to side and add a sufficient amount to make the seams.

When using canvas, only one thickness is necessary. With other fabrics, use two thicknesses plus an interlining, if necessary, for strength.

If working with material that needs strengthening, cut the front, back, and interlining fabric (if used) to the same size. Place the front and back right sides together and place interlining on top. Machine-stitch through all three thicknesses leaving an opening on one side large enough to turn the fabric right side out. Trim fabric close to the stitching line, turn right side out, and press flat, tucking in raw edges of the unsewn opening. Topstitch close to the edges along the two sides. At the ends, fold under the pocket seam allowance and make two rows of stitches close together, backstitching a little at the ends.

Insert the dowels and slide in the seat cover. Slip the back cover over the chair rails and your chair is finished, ready for action.

*If they are to be used outdoors, make sure that covers for director's chairs are made out of sturdy, weather-resistant canvas.*

# DECK CHAIR SLINGS

*D*eck chairs are simple, basic chairs suitable for indoor as well as outdoor use. The frame is generally natural wood, but is easy to paint.

If the chairs will be used in the yard or on a deck, canvas is the recommended choice for the sling. It is the most durable fabric and comes in appropriate widths. With canvas, the sling can be just one thickness. If using material that is not as strong,

plan on two layers plus an interlining for added strength. For indoor use, you have a lot more fabric options, but avoid woven materials, which will stretch or sag.

The most common attachment method is to slip dowels or wooden supports into seam pockets sewn at each end. Not all deck chairs are constructed in this way, however, so when you remove the old sling, pay careful attention to how it was applied. Use the detached sling as a guide for cutting and measuring the new one. Adjust the measurement if the old sling seems somewhat stretched. Remember to add seam

allowances to the sides if you will be using more than one thickness.

If working with material that needs strengthening, cut the front, back, and interlining fabric (if used) to the same size. Place front and back right sides together and interlining on top. Machine-stitch through all three thicknesses, leaving one end open to turn the fabric right side out. Trim fabric close to the stitching line, turn right side out, and press flat, tucking in raw edges of the unsewn end. Topstitch close to edges along the two sides. At ends, fold under the pocket seam allowance and make two rows of stitches close together.

*Make deck chair slings out of fabric that is strong enough to support the weight of a person.*

# OTTOMANS

The method described here for recovering an ottoman is unorthodox but efficient. Before you put on the new cover, you may want to add batting to the cushion if it has become flattened.

## Ottoman with Skirt

Measure top surface, adding seam allowances to all your measurements. Measure boxing pieces, which will be cut separately and sewn together at corners. For boxing depth, measure from top of cushion to the point where cushion meets either welting or padded section.

Measure two lengths of welt cord—one for where boxing joins skirt, the other for the top.

Measure reminder of drop from boxing to floor, adding top seam allowance and 3 inches for hem. For skirt, which will also be cut in four sections, measure width from corner to corner, adding 4 inches plus seam allowances to each piece. Cut out sections and make welt cord.

Begin attaching pieces by sewing welt cord around top of ottoman, clipping corners. Sew the four sections of boxing together at corners, and press open seam.

Sew boxing to top section, and sew welt cord to bottom of boxing.

To make skirt, sew the four sections together at each corner. Press open seam. To make pleats, fold back 2 inches on either side of each corner seam, making a fold that is centered on seam line. Press. On wrong side of skirt, sew three-quarters of the way down, following pressed fold line. Backstitch. Fold pleats back again so that they are centered, and baste top to keep them in place.

Sew this whole section to bottom of boxing, to which welt has already been attached.

Turn up hem, turning in ½ inch and pressing, then turning in another 2½ inches and pressing. Pin or baste and hand-stitch all around. Give cover a final pressing and slide it over ottoman, adjusting it to fit tightly around bottom of cushion area and positioning welt cord correctly.

## Ottoman with Legs

Take measurements as previously described, but for "skirt," cut four sections omitting the additional 4 inches at side seams for pleats, adding simply the seam allowances.

Sew as before until reaching skirt. Then sew the four sections together at corner seams and add to bottom of boxing (which already has welt cord attached). Turn cover right side out and press.

Slip cover over ottoman, adjusting welt cord around bottom of cushion. Pull cover down very firmly.

Turn ottoman upside down in order to work on underside. Clip and shape around legs if necessary, turning under all raw edges. Attach fabric to underneath wooden rail with a staple gun or tacks.

The fabric around the legs will be turned under but not stapled or tacked in the visible areas, so be sure to secure it tightly at both sides of the legs in the hidden underneath rail.

*A crisply tailored ottoman features inverted pleats at the corners.*

# FOLDING SCREENS

*M*aking a screen is a decorative solution to the problem of concealing a clothes rack, interior plumbing, an ugly radiator, or anything you just haven't found a storage place for yet.

A screen can be made to any height, and the length can be adjusted by adding additional panels. Proportionally, three panels 16 inches wide by 72 inches tall form a good-size screen. This size also enables you to cover all three panels out of one width of 54-inch-wide fabric.

If you choose a patterned fabric, be aware that perfect side matching will be impossible because you will be wrapping each panel around the edges of the frames. Covering the back of the screen with fabric is optional, though it does give a more professional finish. Also, you can cover the back in a different fabric so that the screen is reversible.

## Making the Panels

The easiest way to make panels for a screen is to buy wooden stretchers that are used to frame artists' canvases. These are available at art-supply stores in a variety of lengths. Just pick pairs in appropriate sizes for the length and width of your panels and slot the mitered corners together.

If you want to shape the panels, use sheets of plywood. Cut with a jigsaw then upholster as described below.

For an inexpensive and lightweight screen, you can also use sheets of solid foam. However, this means that you must glue rather than staple on the cover and tape rather than hinge the panels together. The advantage is that foam is easy to cut with a knife should you want to shape the panels.

## Covering the Panels

Join frames together. Using a hammer, tap corners lightly to be sure that the tongues are properly seated. Check that frames are perfectly square, then either drive a nail through the corners or put a few staples over them.

Cut fabric into three equal widths of no less than 18 inches each. If you have to use part of the selvage, make sure it will not show on the front or sides. Selvages vary in width, so measure carefully before cutting.

### Covering the Front

Lay fabric face down on a flat surface. Carefully position the frame on top, making sure there is enough fabric on all sides to wrap around frame. Pull fabric around frame and hold it in position with one staple placed in the middle of each side. (If you do not plan to cover the back, turn raw edges under when stapling fabric in place.)

Starting in the middle of one long side, staple fabric at approximately 1-inch intervals. Stop 2 inches away from corners. Fasten fabric to opposite side in the same way, pulling a little as you go. Be careful not to pull so much that you bow the frame. Repeat on top and bottom edges.

Finish corners by making double pleats; staple them in place. Cover all frames in the same way.

### Covering the Back

Spread fabric for back face down on a flat surface. Carefully position frame on fabric with the covered side facing up. Starting in the middle of one long side, fold the raw edge under enough so that fabric edge matches frame edge or is inset about ½ inch. (The depth of the reveal is a matter of choice, but be sure to make it an equal amount on all sides. Also be sure to cover staples holding front fabric in place.) Staple in place, working from the middle toward the

corners. Stop stapling about 2 inches away from corners.

When one side is attached, work on the opposite side, pulling fabric a little as you go. Attach remaining two sides in the same way.

Fold in corners, trimming off excess fabric so that they lie flat. Staple in place.

For a professionally finished look, glue on a frame of trim, tape, or ribbon to cover the staples. Miter-cut all four corners.

## Joining the Panels

Individual panels are hinged together to form a screen with hinges placed on inside edges.

Attach two hinges to first panel. One should be 16 inches down from the top, the other 16 inches up from the bottom. Place hinge in position and mark where screw holes fall. It is advisable to make pilot holes to avoid splitting the wooden frame. If you use pilot holes, first separate fabric threads with a needle or the point of a nail. If you drill through the fabric, you run the risk of getting it wrapped around the drill bit and tearing.

Attach the other two hinges to center panel in the same way. If you have more than three panels, first attach all hinges to individual panels, making sure that hinge plates bend in the right direction. This method makes it easier to align all panels when attaching them together. Stack individual panels on top of each other, making sure they are aligned at the bottom. Mark and drill screw holes as described above, and screw panels together to form the screen.

If the fabric cover has a few wrinkles, spray screen lightly with water using a plant mister. Do not touch it until completely dry. The water will shrink the fabric slightly and smooth out the wrinkles.

*Four padded and fabric-covered panels are hinged together to form a screen that softens the corner of a room and baffles drafts.*

# METRIC CHART

## U.S. Measure and Metric Measure Conversion Chart

| | | Formulas for Exact Measures | | | | Rounded Measures for Quick Reference | | |
|---|---|---|---|---|---|---|---|---|
| | Symbol | When you know: | Multiply by | To find: | | | | |
| **Mass (Weight)** | oz | ounces | 28.35 | grams | | 1 oz | | = 30 g |
| | lb | pounds | 0.45 | kilograms | | 4 oz | | = 115 g |
| | g | grams | 0.035 | ounces | | 8 oz | | = 225 g |
| | kg | kilograms | 2.2 | pounds | | 16 oz | = 1 lb | = 450 g |
| | | | | | | 32 oz | = 2 lb | = 900 g |
| | | | | | | 36 oz | = 2¼ lb | = 1000 g (1 kg) |
| **Volume** | tsp | teaspoons | 5.0 | milliliters | | ¼ tsp | = 1/24 oz | = 1 ml |
| | tbsp | tablespoons | 15.0 | milliliters | | ½ tsp | = 1/12 oz | = 2 ml |
| | fl oz | fluid ounces | 29.57 | milliliters | | 1 tsp | = 1/6 oz | = 5 ml |
| | c | cups | 0.24 | liters | | 1 tbsp | = ½ oz | = 15 ml |
| | pt | pints | 0.47 | liters | | 1 c | = 8 oz | = 250 ml |
| | qt | quarts | 0.95 | liters | | 2 c (1 pt) | = 16 oz | = 500 ml |
| | gal | gallons | 3.785 | liters | | 4 c (1 qt) | = 32 oz | = 1 liter |
| | ml | milliliters | 0.034 | fluid ounces | | 4 qt (1 gal) | = 128 oz | = 3¾ liter |
| **Length** | in. | inches | 2.54 | centimeters | | ⅜ in. | = 1 cm | |
| | ft | feet | 30.48 | centimeters | | 1 in. | = 2.5 cm | |
| | yd | yards | 0.9144 | meters | | 2 in. | = 5 cm | |
| | mi | miles | 1.609 | kilometers | | 2½ in. | = 6.5 cm | |
| | km | kilometers | 0.621 | miles | | 12 in. (1 ft) | = 30 cm | |
| | m | meters | 1.094 | yards | | 1 yd | = 90 cm | |
| | cm | centimeters | 0.39 | inches | | 100 ft | = 30 m | |
| | | | | | | 1 mi | = 1.6 km | |
| **Temperature** | °F | Fahrenheit | 5/9 (after subtracting 32) | Celsius | | 32° F | = 0° C | |
| | | | | | | 68°F | = 20°C | |
| | °C | Celsius | 5/9 (then add 32) | Fahrenheit | | 212° F | = 100° C | |
| **Area** | in.² | square inches | 6.452 | square centimeters | | 1 in.² | = 6.5 cm² | |
| | ft² | square feet | 929.0 | square centimeters | | 1 ft² | = 930 cm² | |
| | yd² | square yards | 8361.0 | square centimeters | | 1 yd² | = 8360 cm² | |
| | a. | acres | 0.4047 | hectares | | 1 a. | = 4050 m² | |

# INDEX